The 100 Funniest Words in English

The 100 Funniest Words in English

in English

Robert Beard

(Dr. Goodword at alphaDictionary.com)

Lexiteria LLC
Lewisburg, Pennsylvania 17837

Library of Congress Control Number: 2009902767

Published by Lexiteria LLC
Lewisburg, Pennsylvania
February 2009
ISBN-13: 978-0-615-26704-3

Contents

Acknowledgements

If no man is an island unto himself, no writer can be. This book would not have come into being in the form it is today without the support of a considerable number of people. Dawn Shawley, my chief lexicographer at Lexiteria, has helped in many ways, not the least of which was proofing the entire manuscript.

Dawn was helped by the editors of alphaDictionary's Good Word series, Paul Ogden, Mary Jane Stoneburg, and Luciano Eduardo de Oliveira, who edit and proof every Good Word we send out, seven days a week. Many of their corrections and suggestions are incorporated in what you are about to read. Paul went the extra mile and read and edited the final manuscript. Responsibility for all remaining errors falls to me, of course.

This book is a by-product of my daily Good Word series; some of the words in this collection originally appeared in that series. The database and interface of that series as it is published daily at alphaDictionary was designed and developed by the systems manager at Lexiteria, Andrew Shaffer. Brian Hilkert also helped indirectly by relieving me of the task of maintaining the finances of Lexiteria for the past three years. This expression of gratitude does not by any means retire my debt to them.

All my ventures have been supported by my wife, Faye, both spiritually and financially. We have been together for over a half century, married most of it. Our sons, Jeffrey and Owen, Owen's adorable wife Collette, and our three grandchildren Laurel, Abigail, and Galen, are the strongest bonds that have ever held two people together. Every day those bonds grow stronger.

Various flukes and scintillae of all these people pervade the following words, invisible, untouchable, but felt deeply by me.

Robert Beard November 2008
Lewisburg, Pennsylvania

Introduction

Words label the bits and pieces of the worlds we live in and it is difficult to understand ourselves and our history without a clear picture of the origins and distributions of these labels. Socrates rightly advised the world that the unexamined life is not worth living. What better way to examine our lives than to examine the words around which we build them? The lives of all human beings are held together by language, so the words we speak must contain deep evidence of who we are, how we think, and where we come from, making them most worthy of examination.

The histories of words are crucial parts of our overall history; they tell us how our thinking has changed and how it has stayed the same. Much of what we know about words is speculative but a serious examination of our vocabulary does help us to a deeper understanding of ourselves and the world we have created around us.

The Good Word series at alphaDictionary.com is an attempt at precisely this. In addition to clarifying issues of pronunciation, spelling, and usage, these 'essaylets,' as I like to call them, demonstrate how these words have been and may be today used creatively. They delve into the history of each word, bringing out the prejudices and thought of English speakers across the ages.

In this book I have tried to sort out a 100 of the funniest words in English from several hundred that are funny for the various reasons discussed in the next section. I hope I've selected your favorites and included some you were unaware of. Tastes, of course, differ; so I ask your indulgence of my choices.

This book separates words that make us laugh and smile from others that affect us differently. This volume, God willing, will be followed by others focusing on other types of words.

Background

Before exploring the humor of the English vocabulary, we need to know a bit about how it stands among the languages of Europe, from which it borrowed more than half its words.

English is a Germanic language, brought to the British Isles by Angles and Saxons around 500 AD from the northern coast of what is today Germany. The original people living in the British Isles, and in northern France as well, were Celts. Celts spoke languages from a different family of languages. It included the various dialects of Gaelic (Irish, Manx, Scottish and Welsh) and Breton, spoken in what is known as Brittany in France today.

French, Italian, Portuguese, and Spanish are Romance languages, so called because they are the remnants of the language spoken in the Roman Empire, Latin. Latin spoken in France became French, Latin spoken in Italy became Italian, and so on.

The Germanic, Celtic, and Romance languages all belong to a greater 'Indo-European' family. It is called this because most of the languages spoken in Europe and India belong to this family. All the languages in Europe except Finnish, Estonian, Turkish, Hungarian, and Basque are Indo-European. Indic languages such as Hindi, Urdu, Marathi, and several other languages spoken in India, belong to the same family.

Linguists have partially reconstructed the original Indo-European language, called 'Proto-Indo-European,' spoken somewhere north of India about 6000 years ago, from which the Indo-European languages may be traced. This is done by comparing words for the same thing in all these languages. For example, the word for "father" in Latin is *pater*, in Greek *pater*, Gothic *fadar*, and in Sanskrit, the ancient language from which modern Indian languages developed, *pitar*.

These are the oldest languages for which we have extensive written evidence. By comparing these words (the comparative method), scientists have explained the rules which operated in order to create the modern languages we have today.

Apparently, the original Proto-Indo-European language contained a word for "father" that was, roughly, *pater*. In the Germanic languages, however, over time, the P became F. This change is then verified by looking at other words in these languages, where we find other evidence of this rule, such as Latin *piscus* and English *fish*, Latin plago "I strike" and English *flog*. Hundreds of such rules have now been established, proving that these languages are all related, descended from one proto-language.

So why are there so many Indo-European languages today, you rightly ask. What happened over the past 6000 or so years is this. As the populace speaking Proto-Indo-European expanded, those farthest from other speakers began pronouncing words slightly differently. The result was the development of accents, then dialects, dialects like those spoken in Australia, the US, and the UK. At first everyone could understand each other, though speakers from one region sounded a bit funny to speakers from another.

As time continued to pass, however, these differences became very deep, to the point that mutual understanding became very difficult and, finally, impossible. At this point, the different dialects became different languages. The same process would then take place again, and again, and again. Languages broke up into dialects, dialects became languages, which soon had dialects, and so on and on and on until we had a wide array of languages across Europe and northern India, languages which now have spread around the world.

Why Words are Funny

We laugh at things that surprise us, catch us off guard in an unthreatening, reassuring manner. If someone says that something we know is beyond their mental capacity or if they say something that doesn't make sense, we laugh. Satire and parody imply stupidity of someone we dislike or hold in low esteem; irony is based on unexpected coincidences. The confusion of two similar words can be hilarious when it results in a pun. Of course, we laugh when we see people do foolish things but most humor arises from conversation, which means it relies heavily on words.

So what makes words funny? A word, naturally, comprises a linguistically distinct sound and at least one meaning. It should come as no surprise, therefore, that words can have funny sounds, funny meanings, and funny combinations of both. So unexpected sounds, meanings, or pairings of the two are occurrences in words that make us smile or laugh.

Of the roughly 6700 languages and dialects in the world, only about 2300 have writing systems and half of those were created primarily for translating the Bible and are not widely used. So, the appearance of the written word plays little role in the humor invested in words. It is mostly the sound, the meaning, or the relation between the two, though funny-sounding words have a way of looking odd, too.

Words with Unexpected Sounds.
The sound of a word can catch us off guard if it seems nonsense but contains a real word inside it. *Flibbertigibbet* and *fuddy-duddy* are two such words. *Gibbet* is actually an archaic English word for "gallows," a sense oddly out of place given the meaning of *flibbertigibbet*. The first component, *flibberti-*, is just a bit of nonsense created on the principles of English word construction but without any meaning by itself.

Fuddy-duddy comprises two nonsense words though, again, both fit the description of a legitimate English word. *Dud* actually is a word and *duddy* is quite similar to *daddy* or *dotty*. This word surprises and delights us because it sounds right and is a little poem that shouldn't mean what it does.

The English education system of the past required all students to learn (well, study) Latin or Greek. The result has been a plethora of English words borrowed from those languages. In the fields of medicine and law, we find thousands of actual Latin words in use. One of the results of this is a sense, especially in the US, that Latin and Greek words are arcane critters reflecting a world of snobbery and unnecessary complication. Poking holes through pretense is the cornerstone of American humor. Parodying things that are made more complicated than they are and elitists who think they are more important than they are always tickles our funny bone.

Creating fake Latin or Latinate (like Latin) words that seem borrowed from Latin for ordinary things is almost a cottage industry, especially in the US, and they are always good for a smile. An example of this kind of funny word is *absquatulate* which only means "to leave," perhaps "abscond." It has a Latin prefix and suffix attached to the rather commonplace English verb *squat*, itself rather funny-sounding. The fact that the meaning of this word means anything but "squat" only deepens the humor. Another example which almost everyone in the US uses is *discombobulate*, again a raft of Latin prefixes and suffixes attached to an unexpectedly simple English word, *bob*.

One other funny sounding (and looking) kind of a word is one, not made from another word, but from a phrase forced into a word's position. I'm thinking now of slang concoctions like *stick-to-itiveness* and *whatchamacallit*. The first one has two legitimate suffixes, *-ive* and *-ness* while the second vaguely resembles one of the many North American Indian words that English has absorbed. Both these words are so well embedded in US English that we hardly notice them now, though they do raise our spirits just a bit when we hear them.

Words with Unexpected Meanings.
Words with unexpected meanings include those whose sound or spelling mislead those who hear it for the first time. An *allegator* is some one who alleges something but it sounds exactly like *alligator*. *Turdiform* suggests something far removed from the thrush it actually refers to. Words like these set the English-speaker up for one meaning, then deliver another. This is usually good for a smile if not a laugh, especially if the spelling of the word suggests something naughty.

In fact, words one letter removed from words with naughty meanings are even funnier than other words with meanings that are simply misleading. The word *crapulence* suggests something worse than "discomfort from overeating or overdrinking," while *formication* "sensation of crawling ants" is only one letter removed from the much, much worse *fornication.* These words are not just funny—they are conversation stoppers.

Sniglets conforming to the rules of English grammar and accepted by a significant portion of the population, usually lift our spirits, too. A sniglet, as comedian Rich Hall defines it, is a word that is not in the dictionary but should be. An example of a funny sniglet is *abibliophobia* based on the Greek root *phobia* "fear." In fact, all the parts of this word are legitimately Greek and are ordered properly. The meaning of this word, however, is one the English language overlooked, for you won't find it in any dictionary: "the fear of running out of reading material."

Sometimes words just have meanings that are funny because they refer to the funny things we humans do. *Gastromancy* may seem to have something to do with romance, but it means "telling the future from stomach rumblings." Just talking about such an activity is funny in itself, regardless of the words you use.

Words with Mismatched Sounds and Meanings.

Other Latinate or Hellenic words are legitimate medical or legal terms which are funny in colloquial English because their classical origin belies the commonness of their meaning. *Rhinorrhea*, for example, simply means "a runny nose." Making fun of elitist overcomplication again. *Lagopodous* means "rabbit-footed," having feet like a rabbit. The humor in these words comes from discovering the surprisingly common meaning coupled with their high-falutin' spelling.

Conclusion.

This pretty much covers the basics of funny words. It is only a brief overview, of course; many details have been omitted that beg further research. I will leave that for others, however, and focus my research on the nature of the words that follow, which I think are the 100 funniest (clean) words in the English language.

Pronunciation Guide

Symbol	Example	Symbol	Example
ah	father, odd	l	let, sell
ai	hide	m	mother
aw	all, walk, caught	n	not (N see below)
ay	day	o	old, stow, though
æ	cab	oo	mood, prude
æw	cow, plough	oy	oil, boy
b	but	p	pen
ch	chin	r	road, wring, rhyme
d	dad	s	say, city
dh	the, either	sh	sheep, nation
e	egg	th	thin, thick
ee	eel, eat, deceit	t	tote
f	fond, phase, laugh	u, uh	about, but, Cuba
g	go, wagon	U	good, would
h	hat	v	very
hw	when	w	wet
i	it	y	yes, n[y]ew
k	key, cat, back	z	zoo, busy
j	jet, geology	zh	vision, azure
N	Nasalized vowel made by opening the nasal passage as in uh-huh [uhN-huhN] "yes."		

NOTE BENE: Glossary

Although most of the linguistic terms used in this book are defined where first used, a glossary of them is included at the end of this book.

Abibliophobia • *Noun*

Pronunciation: uh-bib-li-uh-**fo**-bee-yuh

Abibliophobia is the fear of running out of reading material, a terrible thought, isn't it?

Since you do not have to worry about this problem so long as you are reading this book, let's examine this joke of a word more closely. That *abibliophobia* is a joke does not preclude it from the English vocabulary; the English vocabulary is full of jokes, jokes that make this work possible. *Abibliophobia* is correctly constructed, so if you wish to use it, you will not be breaking any rules of English grammar. This word has derivational relatives: those suffering from abibliophobia are abibliophobes, who are abibliophobic and behave abibliophobically (the adverb).

The easiest scientific words to construct out of the blue are those with the Greek root *-phobia*. Just look up the Greek word for whatever you are afraid of, replace the ending with -o, and couple the results with *-phobia*: "Rita Book suffers from such abibliophobia that she almost lives in the library." Rita's twin sister, Rhoda, claims that she began writing novels as a result of suffering from acute abibliophobia.

This amusing vocabulary item is composed of the Greek prefix a- "not" + bibli-(on) "book" + o + phob(os) "fear" + ia, a nominal suffix. *Biblion* originally referred to a small book or even a scroll. The word for *Bible* in most European languages comes from the plural of this word, biblia "books;" in other words, the original meaning was "The Books," referring to the various manuscripts that were combined to form the Bible.

Absquatulate • *Verb*

Pronunciation: ahb-**sqwah**-chuh-layt

Absquatulate is to take off, bug out, hit the road, make tracks, to blow, get lost and, maybe even to abscond with something.

As you can see in the definition of this word, you don't need squat to absquatulate. In fact, there is quite a bit of disagreement over what this verb actually means. The only sure meaning is what we see above in the definition. The word has been Latinized enough to presume a family of relations like *absquatulation*, *absquatulator*, and *absquatulative*. Just remember that all of them are facetious.

If you find it difficult to get someone to leave you alone and you want to get their attention, try: "Benny, I'm tired of telling you to leave me alone; now, absquatulate before I do something drastic." The word itself should frighten Benny away. Since this word begins with the prefix ab- "away (from)," it has been used in the sense of "abscond": "Duffy seems to have absquatulated with my date while I was in the bathroom; would you like to dance?" Probably not with anyone who talks like that.

Absquatulate was dreamed up in the middle of the 19th century by connecting the Latin prefix *ab-* "away (from)" to the English verb *squat* and a couple more Latin suffixes to make it sound highly technical: legal or medical, I would say. 19th century America produced a lot of fake Latin words, including *argufy*, *citify*, *uppity*, *stick-to-it-ive*, and so on. This funny word is simply another to add to the pile. They reflect the deep-running American suspicion of technical or fancy language.

Allegator • *Noun*

Pronunciation: æ-luh-gay-dur

An **allegator** is an alleger, someone who alleges, who claims something to be true, especially if the claim lacks proof.

Allegator comes from a synonym of *allege*: *to allegate*. The latter rarely rises to the surface of conversation but it does exist. It has an interesting agent noun, *allegator*, that indicates the doer of the deed. Even if it is rarer than *alleger*, it certainly has more potential for play, given its homophone, *alligator*.

Now, when you are subjected to false allegations, you have a more emotionally charged word for your accusers: "Ben Downe is nothing but a cold-blooded allegator who made up the whole story about me putting the frog in the water cooler." How's that for an image of your accuser? Around the house? Sure: "Mom, I am not picking on Billy; he is just an irresponsible allegator." Now, doesn't this word cast a much more powerful beam than commonplace *liar*?

This word is a creation from Latin *allegat(us)*, the past participle of the verb allegare "to send off, relate, recount." The verb comprises ad- "(up)to" + legare "to appoint, assign." So, the prefix *al-* here is really *ad-*, whose consonant becomes like any other consonant to which it is attached (*arrest, attest, adduce* also contain a hidden *ad-*). The primitive root, *leg-/log-*, gave us Latin lex, legis "law" and Greek logos "speech, word, idea." The best guess as to how these two meanings crossed paths is that this root goes back to the day when a king's word was the law and his subjects were as good as their word.

Anencephalous • *Adjective*

Pronunciation: æn-en-**se**-fuh-lus

To be anencephalous is to be brainless, empty-headed, to have a skull with an echo.

It is always more polite to use the medical term for an offensive idea. Here is the medical term for "brainless." It has the added benefit that those you would use it for will not understand it! It offers a wonderful way to vent your frustration inoffensively while building your vocabulary. What a bargain! It comes from the noun anencephaly "the absence of a brain."

We are all constantly bumping into people who seem to have nothing in their heads, many of whom drift into positions of considerable power: "I don't know how many anencephalous presidents this company can endure and stay solvent." We may safely extend the meaning of this word to the product of the witless: "Have you read the latest anencephalous memo from headquarters, the one about saving electricity by not using electric pencil sharpeners?"

This funny word is a Latinization of Greek *anenkephalos*, used by the great 2nd century Greek physician Galen. It is made up of four elements, a(n)- "without" + en "in" + kephale "head" + an adjective suffix. We find the prefix *a(n)-* in many borrowed English words like *amoral, amorphous* (without shape), and *agnostic*. The N is inserted before vowels, as it is when using the English article *a(n)*, as *an apple*. *En* comes from the same source as English *in*. Greek kephale "head" comes from the same Proto-Indo-European word as English *gable* and German Giebel "gable."

Argle-bargle • *Noun*

Pronunciation: ahr-gul-bahr-gul

This bit of British slang refers to an argument, a row, a disputatious bandying of words back and forth between two people.

Argle-bargle is widely used in the UK, as its many variants attest: *argy-bargy*, *argie-bargie*, *argue-bargue*, or simply *argy*, or *bargy*. These forms suggest a diminished importance of the arguing referred to, which is to say, an argument that shouldn't be taken seriously, a spat. However, it belongs to the realm of slang and hence should not be used in your college applications.

The thrust of *argle-bargle* is a mild argument, even a civil debate: "Archie should have been a lawyer rather than a salesman; he enjoys the argle-bargle of contract negotiation more than closing the deal." Since this funny word is colloquial rather than formal, you can push the envelop of English grammar a bit when you use it. Mom might warn the kids, "OK, kids, cut the argy-bargy before it becomes pushy-hitty."

This funny word is a nonsense rhyming compound (like *willy-nilly*, *piggly-wiggly*, *boogie-woogie*) made up of two rhyming words. Their history is interesting: *argle* emerged in the 16th century as a blend of *argue* and *haggle*. *Bargle* was added much later, in the early 19th century, simply because it rhymes with *argle*. The spelling has varied between what you see here and a slightly Greekier *argol-bargol*, but the spelling given here is now the most widely used.

Batrachomyomachy • *Noun*

Pronunciation: buh-træ-kuh-mai-**om**-uh-ki

If you want to say "a tempest in a teacup," "a mountain of a molehill," "making a federal case of a minor issue," but utter it in a single word (not necessarily a single breath), **batrachomyomachy** is the word that does it.

Appropriately enough, this word is a mountain of a mouthful expressing a mole hill of meaning. If you are brave enough to toss it into a conversation, you might as well know the adjective and agent noun. You may be the first to ever use the adjective: *batrachomyomachian* [buh-truh-kuh-mai-o-**may**-ki-un]. Those who exaggerate the importance of things, are *batrachomyomachists* [buh-truh-kuh-mai-**om**-uh-kists]. Honest.

Disputes over trivia occur far too often: "April Showers is raising another batrachomyomachy over the color of the new drapes in the teachers' lounge." Those willing to wait for you to finish uttering this seven-syllable mouthful may be less common: "I don't understand this whole batrachomyomachy over who gets Mona's parking place now that she's gone."

This funny if rather long word is a Greek word meaning "The Battle of Frogs and Mice." It is the title of a mock-heroic epic poem about the struggle between frogs and mice by a small pond, described in the same terms as the siege of Troy is described in *The Odyssey*. The Greek word comes from batrachos "frog," mys "mouse," and machia "fighting," a word related to English *might*, *machine*, and *magic*. *Mys* is the of the same origin as Latin *mus*, whose diminutive, musculus "a little mouse," turned into French *muscle*, whence it made its way to English. Did you know that lifting weights can make you, etymologically speaking, mousy?

Billingsgate • *Noun*

Pronunciation: **bi**-lingz-gayt

Billingsgate is abusive language, scathing profanity applied with a vengeance—or a woman who uses it.

The Billingsgate Fish Market in London is the only fish market I know of that is the eponym of an English word. Historically, Billingsgate has been known as much for the salty language of its fishwives as for its scaly wares. Today it is located in a modern new building where most of the sales staff speak a more palatable idiom. Still, *Billingsgate* is a word that ties us vividly to our history. It is no longer capitalized when used in the sense above.

My dear reader, of course, would never indulge in billingsgate but the word does provide an ear-catching, homespun alternative to such words as *cursing* and *profanity*: "If I ever hear that kind of billingsgate emerge from your mouth again, you will be grounded for life!" (Apparently a family that has banned the death penalty.) If billingsgate is anything, it is an attention-grabber: "I'd love to watch football with you guys Saturday but three hours of billingsgate from Constance Waring is more than I can take."

Billingsgate was originally one of the two water-gates from the Thames to London. It is located just below London Bridge. In 1699 Elizabeth I declared it "an open place for the landing and bringing in of any fish, corn, salt stores, victuals and fruit...." In *Vanity Fair* Thackeray wrote "Mr. Osborne...cursed Billingsgate with an emphasis worthy of the place," and by 1799 even Thomas Jefferson was writing: "We disapprove the constant billingsgate poured on them officially." Your turn.

Bloviate • *Verb, intransitive*

Pronunciation: **blo**-vee-ayt

Bloviate is to speechify using too many highfalutin' words; to speak or write verbosely, like a wind-bag or blow-hard.

This funny word is so well-constructed that many people are fooled into thinking it is real. However, since fanciful words like this one are often accepted (they do add spice to our speech), you should feel free to use it in conversations. *Bloviate* has survived long enough to have earned considerable respectability and raised a family that includes an action noun, *bloviation*, an actor noun, *bloviator*, and an adjective, *bloviating*.

If you bloviate, you bloviate about something or on some topic: "There goes Gene Poole bloviating about his royal ancestry again." Bloviation can be a symptom of obfuscation: "The financial report begins well enough but ends up bloviating about the economic theories of the CFO."

This funny word emerged in the middle of the 19th century as a mock-Latin word. It is based on the English verb *blow* with its associations with blow-hard "braggart" and blow smoke "brag, deceive." The Latinate suffix *-iate* was then tacked on to add to the sense of the highfalutin'. The English word *blow* developed naturally via Old English blawen, akin to *bladder*, *blister*, and *blast*. It has nothing to do with Latin.

Blunderbuss • *Noun*

Pronunciation: blun-dur-bus

No, a **blunderbuss** is not an off-target kiss nor a bus that misses a stop now and then. It is an old-fashioned, short, muzzle-loading musket with a flared muzzle, known for its wide but inaccurate dispersal of shot. It may also refer to a clumsy, bumbling person.

The plural of this word is *blunderbusses*. You can blunderbuss things by simply firing a blunderbuss at them or by going about something in a hit-and-miss fashion. A person who puts a blunderbuss to use is a *blunderbussier*, with a rather sophisticated suffix for such a clumsy word.

Blunderbuss is widely used metaphorically to indicate a random activity or a pattern lacking focus: "Since Percival wasn't familiar with the special-interest groups in the state, he staged a blunderbuss campaign hoping to reach some of the right people." If you tire of calling the dunderheads in your life "dunderheads," this word offers a change of pace: "Lucinda Head is such a hare-brained blunderbuss, she thinks Greece is the capital of Turkey."

This funny word is very rough copy of Dutch *donderbus* from donder "thunder" + bus "box, gun." Dutch *donder*, German *Donner*, and English *thunder* all came from the same original root. The Dutch word *bus* is related to the Latin word *buxis* with the same meaning (English *box* is also a kinsword). The problem for English speakers is that *donder* isn't an English word, so it's no wonder that we replaced *donder* with *blunder*, not an inappropriate substitution for such a clumsy gun. This process, called 'folk etymology,' is a historical change that follows folk intuition rather than grammatical rules.

Borborygm • *Noun*

Pronunciation: bor-buh-ri-gum

A **borborygm** is a grumbling of the bowels, the rumbling of the stomach such as might occur before or after eating a heavy meal.

If you wish to speak medically, you can call this embarrassing sound a *borborygmus*—just remember that the plural of this word is *borborygmi*. If you use our shortened form, you may simply say *borborygms* for the plural. The adjective for either form is *borborygmic* and *borborology* is the scientific study of the phenomenon. If you don't want your borborygms to go to waste, you might try a little after-dinner gastromancy (page 55), fortune-telling based on stomach grumblings. Yep, that is part of our past, too.

Borborygm is the perfect word for the sound it names, a fact that has attracted writers for ages. Aldous Huxley complained about "the stertorous borborygms of the dyspeptic Carlyle" and Vladimir Nabokov noted in one of his novels that "all the toilets and water pipes in the house had been suddenly seized with borborygmic convulsions." Elizabeth Fenwick wrote metaphorically in *Long Way Down* (1959), "The room was very quiet, except for its borborygmic old radiator."

This funny word came to us from Greek *borborygmos* via Latin to French *borborygme*, where English picked it up. It is clearly onomatopoetic, the imitation of a real sound in the sound of the word that names it. It is odd that the French and English did not simplify this word to *borborism*, as the Greeks themselves ultimately did.

Boustrophedon • *Noun*

Pronunciation: bus-truh-**fayd**-un

Boustrophedon is a back-and-forth style of writing used by the Hittites and ancient Greeks, in which the lines are written alternately from left to right, then back again, right to left. Some typesetting software operates by boustrophedon to save time. Just before the line printer was invented, some early computer output printers had boustrophedonic heads that moved left to right, then right to left, again, for speed.

In the 2000 US federal elections, the (in)famous butterfly ballots used in Florida that listed candidates on facing pages, were called by some *boustrophedonic*, the adjective for this peculiar word. The metaphor does not quite work but those who know this word would make the connection. The adverb is boustrophedonically "in a back and forth pattern."

Systematic searches often follow a boustrophedon: "We carried out a very careful boustrophedonic search of the wooded area and found nothing." Heating elements and cooling coils in refrigerators are often boustrophedonic, and boustrophedonic ribbon candy is not at all rare.

This funny word comes from Greek boustrophedon "turning like an ox (while plowing)," a compound containing bous "ox" + strophe "a turning." *Bous* originated in the Proto-Indo-European word gwou- "cow, bull, ox" which reached English as *cow*, Hindi as *gaya* (Sanskrit *gauh*), and shows up in Russian govyadina "beef." We also find the Greek *bous* tucked into boubalos "buffalo," an ancestor of English *buffalo*. *Strophe* comes from the Greek verb strephein "to turn" and is a relative of English *strap* and Latin stroppus "twisted cord."

Bowyang • *Noun*

Pronunciation: bo-yæng

A **bowyang** is a gaiter or strap, usually made of leather, tied around the trouser leg just below the knee. This word can also refer to a short chap that covers the leg from the knee to the ankle like overboots.

More interesting than the usage of this funny word (it is used exclusively in Australia) is the usage of the bowyangs themselves. Outbackers love to tell you that they are worn to prevent snakes from crawling up your trousers. Others say they keep insects and similar vermin out of the pants. They probably were originally used to prevent the pants from riding down while ranchers were shearing sheep.

Whatever the reason for them, they symbolize the yokel to Australians: "Clarence stood against the wall during the entire dance without saying anything, like a farmer out for the first time without his bowyangs." Bowyangs in the second sense of this word are useful whenever you are gardening or doing dirty work close to the ground: "If you want me to clean the kids' room, you'll have to get me a pair of bowyangs."

This funny word can only be traced back to the dialects of Scotland and Northern England, where you find words like *bowy-yanks* and *bow-yankees* referring to leather leggings. In Scotland you also hear *booyangs* and *bonanks*. The implication might be that they are pieces of clothing that you yank on and perhaps tie in a bow. However, this is pure speculation where speculation is all we have to go on.

❧

Brouhaha • *Noun*

Pronunciation: broo-hah-hah

A **brouhaha** is a hubbub, commotion, uproar; it is an embarrassing scandal, a big stink that causes a lot of talk.

This word is so odd and isolated that it has no lexical relatives other than plural *brouhahas*. Do make sure you place the accent on the first syllable and not the second, where it would more naturally fall in English. Also be sure to include the O since this word is often misspelled *bruhaha*. It might help to remember that even though beer may lead to a brouhaha, the spelling *brewhaha* should also be avoided except in jest.

Brouhahas are closely associated with sporting events in the US: "No one was laughing after the brouhaha that erupted when the umpire called Wiley Slider out at home plate." Any excited contentious situation may be characterized as a brouhaha: "Yes, there was quite a family brouhaha when Sue Barew came home with the nose tattoo and a lip ring."

This funny word comes from 16th century French *brouhaha*, taken from a chant by a priest disguised as the devil in a late 15th century French farce: "Brou brou brou ha ha, brou ha ha!" It is possible that the playwright simply made up sounds imitating confused speech. But it is also very possible that it comes from the Hebrew phrase barukh habba "blessed be he who enters," frequently heard in Jewish ceremonies and suspiciously similar to barruccaba "hubbub" in Italian dialects. When most school children studied Latin and Greek, Hebrew to them was the equivalent of Greek in the English idiom "it's all Greek to me." The derivation would then parallel that of English *patter*, which came from Latin pater noster "our Father."

Bumbershoot • *Noun*

Pronunciation: bum-bur-shoot

A **bumbershoot** is an umbrella or parasol, especially an old-fashioned one.

This word is one of the many nonsense words acceptable now in colloquial US English along with *gobbledegook, snollygoster, stick-to-it-iveness*, and most of the other words in this book. Remember that it ends in *-shoot* even though the origin of the pronunciation is probably that of *-chute* (see below).

Many Americans will remember this word from the song, "Me ol' bam-boo" in the movie *Chitty Chitty Bang Bang*:

> Me ol' bam-boo, me ol' bam-boo
> You'd better never bother with me ol' bam-boo
> You can have me hat or me bum-ber-shoo
> But you'd better never bother with me ol' bam-boo.

Today this word may be used more often in reference to the Seattle art and music festival, *Bumbershoot*. The festival received this name because it is an umbrella festival for all the arts in Seattle rather than as a reference to that city's weather.

The origin of this word is fairly obvious though no one knows for sure who created it or when. It seems to be a compromise between the beginning of *umbrella* (*umber*), with a replication of the B, plus the end of *parachute*. It was first remarked in 1896 in the *Random House Historical Dictionary of the American Language* even though most Americans associate it with the British upper class. In fact, it is generally unknown in the UK. It is remindful of a child's mispronouncing *umbrella* as *underbrella*, as my son did when he was a child.

☙

Callipygian • *Adjective*

Pronunciation: kæ-luh-**pi**-jee-un

Callipygian means having or pertaining to a well-proportioned, shapely rear end (buttocks). Hmmm.

This funny though felicitous word expresses our appreciation of the human anatomy, which tends to be fixed on a few specific regions. Not only is this word a polite way to refer to this alluring physiognomic characteristic but a euphonious (pleasant-sounding) one, to boot.

This is a word we can all use fearlessly, "The ever-observant Marian Kine lingered a slight moment in the bookstore to more fully calculate the callipygian young man reaching for tomes on the upper shelves." Age can damage or improve this characteristic of our bodies: "The passing years had remolded Gloria Sass's figure into that of a zaftig woman of eminent callipygian luxuriance."

This funny but lovely word is based on Greek *kallipygos*, a compound comprising kallos "beauty" + pyge "buttocks." Neither of these words seems to have roots. *Kallos* could hardly be related to Latin *callus* "hardened skin" and, although it resembles English *hallow*, most etymologists (word historians) think *hallow* is unrelated. If *pyge* were related to any English word, it would be an obscenity in our beloved language. As such, it would not have been printed until recently, since the media made obscenities fashionable, making tracing its history impossible.

Canoodle • *Verb*

Pronunciation: kuh-**noo**-dul

Canoodle means to bill and coo, to spoon, to pet, or make out. To canoodle is to cuddle up with someone you are most fond of.

Over the past centuries every generation has had a different word or phrase for engaging in this universally enjoyable and enjoyed activity. This one is seldom heard outside the northeastern US these days, but it is worth saving. The spelling of this word has been Anglicized as *canoodle*, even though its origin is the Yiddish verb *knuddeln*. People who canoodle are canoodlers enjoying a bit of canoodlery (or canoodling).

Though this word still sounds too slangy for formal English, it is a cute, mildly funny word for this activity: "Buffy was stunned to find her parents canoodling on the very living room couch that she and her boyfriend, Biff Stroganoff, had hoped to put to the same use." The derivations are just as funny as the basic verb: "The canoodlers were tied in a knot sealed at the lips by a kiss."

This word did not originate with an image of noodles knotted together, even though this image might have crossed your mind as you read the definition and examples above. It is yet another one of those words English borrowed from Yiddish (and never returned). Yiddish picked the word up from German knuddeln "to hug, pet." English speakers do not handle the consonant combination KN at the beginning of a word as well as Yiddish speakers, so we added the vowel A and converted the K to a C, no doubt to disguise the fact that this word really belongs to another language.

Cantankerous • *Adjective*

Pronunciation: kæn-**tæng**-kur-us

Cantankerous means quarrelsome, ill-tempered, crotchety, ornery, hard to put up with. It can also mean difficult to handle or control, as a cantankerous old computer.

A verb *cantanker* has recently been extracted from this adjective, so now we can say that *cantankerous* is the adjective of the verb *cantanker* "to be cantankerous." The adverb is *cantankerously* and the noun is simply *cantankerousness*—but why not *cantankerosity* in the spirit of *generosity*? The verb *cantanker* also led to a newer adjective, *cantankersome*, and left the door wide open for a personal noun, *cantankerer*.

Despite the large family that has emerged around this silly word, it is still felt to be too slangy for formal English. It is perfectly acceptable in conversation, though: "Burney Bottoms is so cantankerous that he complains when the kids are too quiet in the house." Things that sometimes work and sometimes don't are also said to have this quality: "Festus bought a cantankerous old pickup that never wants to start during hunting season!"

Cantankerous is cantankerous itself in that it refuses surrender its origin or any clues about it. It is probably a tangle of bits and pieces from *contentious*, *rancorous*, and *cankerous*. As mentioned before, English speakers in the US take a dim view of '50-cent' words, especially if they are Latinate, and often make up funny ones just to ridicule their likes.

Catercornered • *Adverb*

Pronunciation: kæ-dur-kor-nurd

Catercornered means to be positioned diagonally across (from), or in the corner diagonally across from the person or thing under discussion. It can also mean to be awry, cocked, or crooked.

This funny member of the English vocabulary is hard to get a handle on. It is sometimes pronounced *catty-cornered*, sometimes *kitty-cornered*. Sometimes the suffix *-ed* is dropped: *catercorner, catty-corner, kitty-corner*. New Englanders appear to have thrown up their hands in frustration over this confusion and have come up with their own word with the same meaning: *antigoggling*. This frustration might also explain the use of *catty-wampus* in the same sense down South.

The classical use of this cute word is to refer to objects situated at opposite corners from each other: "Nadeen's house is situated catercornered from ours on the intersection of Redneck Drive and Chuck Wagon Circle." It can indicate that something is positioned at an angle: "Mama said to straighten up the couch; she doesn't like it sitting catercornered (antigoggling, catty-wampus) in the room like that."

This word arose when French quatre "four" was borrowed and written as *catre*. It applied to the 'four' side of a die (plural *dice*). *Catercorner* originally meant "having dots in each of four corners." *Cater* was then tacked on to the front end of several English words, including *catercap*, a four cornered hat that was worn askew, with corners pointing fore and aft. Since no one really knew what *cater* meant, some apparently took it to mean "askew" and, voila! *catercornered* as it is used today.

Cockalorum • *Noun*

Pronunciation: kahk-uh-**lor**-rum

A **cockalorum** is a little man with a disproportionately high opinion of himself, who crows about himself a lot. This word can also refer to the crowing itself, in other words, cockamamie cockalorum can be uncontrolled boasting, false self-praise.

Now, everyone will tell you that the plural of this funny word is *cockalorums*. However, since the word itself is a joke, why not push it to the limits and call a bunch of cocky twerps cockalora? The reference also seems to be to bantam roosters, for the sense of this word is usually restricted to small men.

We don't like to encourage the use of pejorative terms but this word is so funny it is hard to resist: "That little cockalorum loves to crow about all the actors he met growing up in Beverly Hills." I further discourage anyone from saying anything like, "The little cockalorum is in the boss's office now giving himself credit for all the changes we made over his protestations." But you can see how someone might ignore my advice.

This word obviously shares a source with *cocky*, referring to someone who prances around as full of himself as a rooster. It has been suggested that it was built upon the base of an obsolete Flemish verb, kockeloeren "to crow." It might just as well have been the result of monkeying around with *cock-a-doodle-doo* and the Latin genitive plural ending, *-orum*. However, the only thing we are sure of is the influence of the Latin ending. The sentiment is related to the old French saying: Le coq est roi sur son fumier "The rooster is king on his dunghill."

Cockamamie • *Adjective*

Pronunciation: kahk-uh-may-mee

Cockamamie means absurd, foolish, outlandish, implausible, crazy, unrelated to reality.

This word was popular in the 1930s and 1940s but its popularity has dipped a bit of late, though we do hear it from time to time. It lives alone without any derivational kinswords.

This is a good word to toss into conversations with your grand-parents, who will remember it with fondness: "Grandpa, where did you get that cockamamie hat you are wearing?" It is such a funny vocabulary item that we should try to pass it on to the next generation, too: "A fox jumped in the front window and caused you to swerve the car into a tree? Do you expect me to believe a cockamamie story like that?!"

In the middle of the 19th Century decals became a mania in Victorian Britain, so much so that Britons borrowed a word from French, decalcomania "mania for decals," to describe it. (Our current word, *decal*, by the way, is a clipping of that word.) The French word, *decalcomanie* "mania for (tombstone) tracings," resulted from the previous mania in Europe. This word is made up of the prefix de- "from, off" + calquer "to copy, trace" + manie "mania." So what has this cockamamie story to do with the word under discussion? *Cockamamie* is, in fact, nothing but a corruption of *decalcomania* that gained currency over the years to become the whimsical slang adjective it is today.

Codswallop • *Noun*

Pronunciation: kahds-wah-lup

Codswallop is bull, bunkum, fiddle-faddle, flapdoodle, horse feathers, hogwash, hooey, hokum, malarkey, poppycock, tommy-rot, whang-doodle, or common everyday windbaggery.

This word, which reeks of the days of Uriah Heap, Mr. Micawber, and the Artful Dodger, is in fact so recent a coinage that it has had no time to build a family. It is so English, however, we can easily project a *codswalloper* who engages in *codswallopery*, not to mention a naked verb: "You know that Hiram Cheaply is cods-walloping if his lips are moving."

It is an unfortunate fact of modern life that we need a steady stream of words meaning "nonsense": "All that talk about Harry Beard's work in the government being top secret is codswallop unless the government keeps his work secret to avoid embarrassment." Of course, governments usually provide the finest in codswallop: "For the best in codswallop, flapdoodle, and gobbledygook, we can now turn to Congress's own TV network, C-SPAN."

One story of the origin of this word would have Hiram Codd patenting a bottle for fizzy drinks with a neck containing a marble that kept the bottle shut until it was pressed inwards. That would have been back in the 19th century. *Wallop* then was a slang word for beer, so *Codd's wallop* could have been used by beer drinkers as a term for bad beer or soft drinks. The problem is that *codswallop* first appeared in print only in the 1950s. Moreover, while the word has been spelled *cod's wallop*, there is no published evidence of any spelling *Codd's wallop*. Conclusion? No one has any idea where this word comes from.

Collop • *Noun*

Pronunciation: kah-lup

A **collop** can be a few things. It may be a slice or chunk of meat or a fold of body flab indicating a well-fed constitution. A collop is also an egg fried on a piece of ham or bacon, especially if eaten on Collop Monday, the day before Shrove Tuesday.

This humorous word is an endangered lexical orphan, homeless, without family, wandering the streets and byways of Scotland and northern England pretty much alone. In the overweight world we currently live in, the word is too relevant to leave to the Scots and the souls of Yorkshire to have all the fun with.

Should your mum ask your pleasure at the dinner table, impress her with this: "Would you pass me three collops of the roast beef with a dollop of mashed potatoes, please." But do not confuse *collop* with dollop "a lump or glob." Their meanings are very close but not synonymous. We don't like to think of collops on ourselves, but they do sometimes appear: "Barb Dwyer is a lovely woman except for the collops under her chin." Pigs are a natural place to find the collops whether in the sty or on the table.

The origin of this word is obscure. It is related to Swedish kalops "beef stew" and German Klops "meatball," though no one knows exactly how. In Scotland it has been used to refer to a dish made of chopped meat called 'Scottish collops' outside Scotland. A better suggestion is that it is a variant of *scallop*, also spelled *scollop* in some parts of the English-speaking world. This word was taken from the French word escalope "shell," which also refers to a slice of meat, perhaps because some meat slices curl like a shell when cooked. Unfortunately, there is no explanation of why English would drop the initial ES from this word.

Collywobbles • *Noun*

Pronunciation: kah-li-wah-bulz

Collywobbles refers to queasiness caused by anxiety, fear, or anticipation, in other words, butterflies in the stomach.

Collywobbles is pretty much out there on its own, without any derivational relatives. It currently requires a plural verb, although in the past it has been used in the singular when referring to actual stomach pain. This noun today may be used with a singular or plural verb: "collywobbles is" or "collywobbles are": your choice.

Now we have a name for those butterflies we get in our stomach that are let in by fear and anxiety: "Gosh, just looking at Sue St. Marie gives me the collywobbles." Collywobbles may be a part of the survival response for it is with us from an early age: "My granddaughter got the collywobbles when she saw Santa Claus for the first time at the mall and never did tell him what she wanted for Christmas."

This funny word is a compound originally made up of *colic* + *wobble* + -s, a suffix associated with ailments (*measles*, *mumps*, *blues*). *Colic* was borrowed from Old French *colique*, the remnant of Latin colica (passio) "colonic (suffering)," feminine of colicus "of the colon." *Colicus* came from *kolikos*, the Greek adjective from kolon "colon." *Wobble* is an authentic English word indicating a vibration or other back and forth movement that was inherited from a root that gave us the Germanic family of words that includes *web*, *waffle*, and *weave*.

Comeuppance • *Noun, mass*

Pronunciation: kum-**up**-unts

Comeuppance means *just deserts* "deserved punishment" (as opposed to "just desserts," when we skip the main course of a meal). The word *deserts* in the sense and spelling used here is an old noun from the verb *deserve*, meaning "that which is deserved."

This acceptable if not really kind word has alternated historically with *come-upping*. The hyphen has had a difficult time finding its place in these words: *come-up-ing*, *come-uppance*, and *come-up-ance* have all been tried. Today it is either omitted altogether or placed after *come*: *come-uppance*.

When we feel that someone receives punishment well deserved, we may call it comeuppance: "Well, that Maud Lynn Dresser got her comeuppance for attending the party so outrageously over-dressed when one of her spiked heels broke and she fell into the pool." It is a slang word, however, so avoid using it in legal documents: "You'll get your comeuppance some day for putting me through such misery!"

This funny word is one that demonstrates just how outrageously English words can be created. *Comeuppance* has the French suffix, *-ance* added to a phrase, *to come up*, rather than to the single word English grammar normally allows. The sense of *come up* in this word is the one it has in the phrase "to come up for judgment." Only English permits such ridiculous self-abuse and it does so regularly; *stick-to-itiveness* and *one-upmanship* are two other examples of the same grammatical travesty. Often we convert phrases to words without affixation. "You are so over-the-top," converts the phrase "over the top" into an adjective without so much as a by-your-leave, let alone a suffix.

Crapulence • *Noun, mass*

Pronunciation: kræ-pyuh-lunts

Crapulence is the discomfort resulting from immoderate eating or drinking. However, some think that crapulence is overeating or overdrinking itself. I don't.

This word has two adjectives, the obvious *crapulent*, plus a synonym, *crapulous*, with adverbs *crapulently* and *crapulously*, respectively. This word is used rarely in medicine in its original Latin sense of "intoxication," but it still serves as a good general substitute for *hangover*.

Now that you know *crapulence* doesn't mean what you thought it meant, you may use it even in polite company: "Thanksgiving dinner was a feast of plenty at our house but it brought on a wicked bout of crapulence that scoffed at every antacid I fed it." Good advice to keep in mind: "If the wages of thin are hunger, the wages of pudge are crapulence."

This funny word comes from Late Latin crapulentus "drunk," an adjective built up from the noun crapula "intoxication." The root of *crapula* is the same as that of Greek kraipale "hangover." It is totally unrelated to *crap*, which comes from the losing throw in the dice game called *craps*, a word donated to English by the French speakers of Louisiana. The 'Cajun' French word was borrowed from English *crabs*, the original name of the dice game. *Crab* is related to *crawl*, an activity often accompanying crapulence from drinking. (The nausea following immoderate indulgence in craps comes from poverty and is also unrelated to *crapulence*.)

Crudivore • *Noun*

Pronunciation: kroo-duh-vor

You have to watch the pronunciation of **crudivore** to avoid implying that someone is an eater of crud. That is not what a crudivore is: a crudivore is someone who eats only raw food.

Crudivorism is a term for a dietary fad that has been spreading around the world and the Web. It refers to the belief that humans are healthier and live better and longer when their food is eaten raw. Some modern crudivores are also vegetarians (herbivores) but many are carnivorous. Following the pattern of similar words, if the belief is *crudivorism*, a person practicing it is a *crudivorist*, but *crudivore* works just as well.

Although this funny word is just creeping into English, and even though it refers to a fringe eating fad, wider applications can be imagined: "Most species are crudivores, so what is the word for a species that eats cooked food?" Once we have made this leap of faith, metaphorical applications pop up all around us: "Barnaby eats his meat so rare we think of him as a borderline crudivore."

This very new word was concocted from Latin crudus "raw, unripe, undigested" + *-vorus*, from vorare "to gobble up, devour." Believe it or not, Latin *crudus* and English *raw* started out as the same word, Proto-Indo-European *kreu- "raw flesh." The initial K quite regularly became Latin C and English H, giving us Old English hreaw "raw." Initial H before consonants vanished in English on the trip to us. Latin added the suffix *-d* plus its own endings and, voila, *crudus*! English took the French variant of that one, too, as *crude*.

Discombobulate • *Verb, transitive*

Pronunciation: dis-kum-**bah**-byuh-layt

Discombobulate means to confuse, befuddle, disconcert or disorient; to throw into mental disarray.

Current dictionaries are still reluctant to discuss the family of this common but still funny word. The action noun for this verb is *discombobulation*, which suffices to demonstrate that the word is fully Latinized. This means that derivations like *discombobulator*, *discombobulative*, and *discombobulable* are fully potential, even though they rankle my spellchecker.

A discombobulative situation would be one in which you wish to indicate befuddlement and get a smile at the same time: "Well, I'm a little discombobulated right now and can't think of an alternative to *discombobulate*." It is not a word you would use in a job interview but elsewhere use it with relish: "When he is in England, Cedric often becomes discombobulated and often drives in the right lane." Well, at least he is still with us.

As with laws of state, we have devised many ways to circumvent the laws of grammar. This funny word probably dropped from someone's lips when they were searching futilely for a word like *discompose*, which they mixed it up with *bobble*, then added the Latin suffix *-ate* in an attempt to cover their tracks. The result is so amusing, however, that it will continue to be repeated so long as it gets a smile each time it is uttered. It first appeared in print in the mid 1930s in the *New York Sun*, making it clear that it is another one of those crazy US lexical concoctions.

Donnybrook • *Noun*

Pronunciation: dahn-i-brUk

A **Donnybrook** is a major melee, a huge public brawl, a riot, total pandemonium. It may also be simply a nasty argument that gets out of control.

Donnybrook is a stand-alone word, a lexical orphan with no derivational relatives. It is written as one word with no hyphen, though. Keep that in mind.

Donnybrooks broke out around the world in 2006 when Muslims rioted in response to a Danish cartoon dealing with Mohammed. You occasionally encounter a donnybrook on the domestic front, too: "In the donnybrook that erupted at the rock concert Lula Mae lost her temper and the left sleeve of her coat."

The annual fair in Donnybrook, Ireland, south of Dublin, was more notable for its brawls than its wares by 1822. In that year a summary of the fair reported "four broken heads, black eyes, bloody noses, squeezed hats, singed, cut and torn inexpressibles, jocks and upper benjamins, loodies, frocks, tippets, reels and damaged leghorns, together with sundry assaults, fibbings, cross buttocks, and ground floorings too numerous to mention." (Please don't ask what all these items are.) The name comes from Irish Domhnach-broc "the Church of Broc." Broc was the name of a woman noted for building a convent in the area in the 8th century.

Doozy • *Noun*

Pronunciation: doo-zee

Most folks think a **doozy** is a pip, a beaut, a lulu, a humdinger, or even a lollapalooza, in other words, an epitome, prime example, something truly extraordinary in its class. However, according to the late great George Carlin, "There are two pips in a beaut, four beauts in a lulu, eight lulus in a doozy, and sixteen doozies in a humdinger. No one knows how many humdingers there are in a lollapalooza." I wouldn't argue with him; I don't think I have ever seen a real lollapalooza. The plural of this word is *doozies*, which leads some speakers to assume that the singular is spelled *doozie*. It isn't.

Lulu is an almost equally funny word but the origin of *lulu* is a doozy of a mystery, so let's settle for *doozy* itself—a lulu of a word, wouldn't you say? If we follow Carlin's formula, we could say things like, "Portia Carr's new Maserati is a doozy of a car." Of course *doozie* is no longer limited to cars: "That lawyer Susan Liddy-Gates has a doozie of a case on her hands!"

The question of the origin of this funny if slangy word has bred two schools of thought. Some think it a corruption of *daisy*, which, in the 19th and early 20th centuries referred to anything first-rate. However, the slippage from the vowel in *daisy* to that in *doozy* is unlikely. Others think this word is a variant of *Duesy*, short for Duesenberg, the expensive and exquisite car of the 20s and 30s. The problem here is that the word *doozy* first appeared in print in 1903. However, prior to building their superb cars, the brothers Duesenberg built superb racing bicycles (raced them, too), and they began that business in 1895. The best speculation, then, is that this funny word began as a clipping of the bicycle name, and was reinforced in the 20s and 30s by the reputation of the car.

Dudgeon • *Noun*

Pronunciation: duh-jun

A **dudgeon** is unrelated to basement prisons, though it might reflect the mood of someone kept in one. It means a huff, a petulant, resentful, or snarky mood, as to fall into a dudgeon over not being promoted.

Because we have largely ignored this poor word since the 17th century, it has not been able to develop a family of derivations. Though it is rarely used as a verb, the *Oxford English Dictionary* still lists it as a verb that might be used alone in sentences like, "Do you have to dudgeon around the house all weekend long, Harold?" Sometimes this word is used with the article 'a': "to be in a high dudgeon" and sometimes without: "to depart in high dudgeon."

Dudgeon is most often associated with unhappy departures and is usually measured on a scale of high to low: "Slamming the door loudly in my face, Lucille leapt into her car and drove away in high dudgeon." We also find dudgeon in the workplace: "Miss Pell resigned in a fuming dudgeon when she was told she could no longer work as a copy editor."

The original form of this funny word seems to have been *endugine*, a word of undisclosed origins. It lost its initial syllable by a common process called 'aphaeresis.' *Endugine* may have come from Welsh dygen "malice, resentment," perhaps with an enhancing prefix *en-* added for some reason lost in the wrinkles of time. If so, it would be related to Cornish duwhan, "grief, sorrow." This is all we know or can guess about it.

CR

Ecdysiast • *Noun*

Pronunciation: ek-di-zee-æst

An **ecdysiast** is an exotic dancer, strip-tease, a person who sheds his or her clothes while dancing.

This word is based on ecdysis "molting," which comes with an adjective, *ecdysial*. We might be able stretch the meaning of this adjective to cover that of *ecdysiast*. It makes more sense, however, to posit an entirely new word family on the order of *ecdysiastic*, *ecdysiastically*, and *ecdysiasm*—all grammatically well-formed though currently unendorsed by most dictionaries.

One of the earliest known ecdysiasts was Salomé, who, according to legend, received the head of John the Baptist in return for a rendition of her seductively ecdysiastic *Dance of the Seven Veil*s. Ecdysiasm has survived the intervening two thousand years: "After flunking out of the ballet academy, Leah Tarde went to work as an ecdysiast and made more money in a year than she would have as a ballerina over a lifetime."

H. L. Mencken has been accorded the honor of creating this word for Miss Georgia Sothern, who asked him for a more dignified name for her profession around 1940. In doing so, Mencken modified a scientific term, ecdysis "molting, casting off," as snakes and crabs molt their old skins or shells as they grow. Ecdysis was merely taken from the Greek ekdysis "stripping off," the noun from ekduein "to take off." This verb comprises ek "out of, off" + duein "to put on, dress." The root that produced *duein* also turns up in Sanskrit upa-du- "put on," but apparently it was not widely developed outside these languages.

Eructation • *Noun*

Pronunciation: uh-ruk-**tay**-shun

An **eructation** is a belch, a burp, or similar release of gases from the stomach through the mouth. Ooops! Excuse me!

For the older generation of English speakers, it remains uncomfortable even to refer to gases emitted from the mouth, so the medical term still has a place in the general vocabulary. The verb underlying this noun, *eructate*, also fathered an adjective, *eructative*. If you ever need this word but want to hurry past it as fast as you can, you may use an older, shorter form, *eruction*. However, this variant is rare now and most dictionaries consider it archaic.

When even the word *burp* makes us feel uncomfortable—and *belch* is way out of the question—the medical term becomes a useful surrogate: "Dinner would have been perfect except for the sudden eructation by Frieda Gogh that marked its conclusion." "Belch forth" is very close to the metaphorical sense of this word: "His meandering talk ended on an eructation of invectives against Michael Moore's documentary films."

This funny word comes from Latin eruct-are "belch out," made up of e(x) "out (of)" + ructare "to belch, emit." You may find the Latin word today not far from its original form and meaning in Italian *eruttare* and in Spanish *eructar*. The verb stem *ruct-* is the Latin derivation of Proto-Indo-European reug- "to vomit, belch," which came through Old Germanic to English as *reek*. In Lithuanian it emerged as raugėti "to belch" and Greek as ereugomai "to vomit." So the word has been around for a long time and has filtered down into practically all Indo-European languages.

Fard • *Noun*

Pronunciation: fahrd

Fard is either ordinary face-paint, make-up or facial cosmetic, or any cover-up or decoration that conceals a fault or imperfection.

In the 18th century English noblewomen applied a white coloring to their faces to conceal the tire prints of time. Today we have other words for facial makeup, but *fard* is still useful in emphasizing make-up that specifically covers blemishes. It may also be used as a verb in the wider sense: "The president uses these weekly socials as a means of farding over the tensions and conflicts that can't be resolved by management."

Now that makeup has staged its comeback after the Sixties, it is time to give this funny word another chance. "Barbie Dahl is such a master at farding her face, you would never dream that her last birthday was her sixtieth." But you must promise to resist the temptation of ever saying anything like, "That old fard-faced Dolly Salvador looks like a clown in all the make-up she wears." I'm already embarrassed to think that I might have encouraged it.

This funny little word comes from French farder "to make up." The stem of this word was probably borrowed from Old High German faro "colored," which went on to become German Farbe "color." An interesting side note: the same root emerged in Latin as *perca* and in Greek as perke "perch." After having been passed on down through several centuries to French, we borrowed it as our word *perch*, a colorful little fish.

CR

Fartlek • *Noun*

Pronunciation: fahrt-lek

A **fartlek** is an athletic training system for endurance sports like bicycling and running, composed of periods of intense exercise separated by periods of less strenuous effort. It could also be an interval in a workout based on this technique.

The saltin fartlek is a fartlek for runners. It is made up of a 10-minute warm-up jog, followed by a 3 minute hard stride followed by a 1-minute jog. The word itself has not completely escaped Swedish and so has not produced a family of English derivations, just a plural, *fartleks*.

Fartleks are best suited for sports that require endurance: "Randy Marathon does a dozen fartleks every day when he trains for a major race." Now that Randy is well over 50, he generally runs with a group known as the Old Fartleks and doesn't compete seriously. However, the alternation of vigorous with slower activity sets the stage for metaphoric manipulation: "Buzzy, you can't study in fartleks; you have to study in long uninterrupted stretches if you hope to graduate."

Gosta Holmer, a Swedish track coach, developed an athletic training technique in the 1930s which he called fartlek "running play" from fart "running" + lek "play." *Fart* comes from Swedish fara "go, run," a reflex of the Old Germanic word that produced German fahren "to travel" and English *fare* in *farewell*. In Greek, the original root emerged as poros "journey," still lurking in English *emporium*, borrowed from Greek emporion "merchant," someone who did quite a bit of journeying in ancient Greek times.

Fatuous • *Adjective*

Pronunciation: fæ-chuh-wus

No, you don't get **fatuous** by overeating or stuffing yourself with carbs. This word means smugly or unconsciously foolish, silly, stupid, the way we may feel when we overeat or stuff ourselves with carbs.

The original pronunciation of this word was [**fæ**-tyu-wuhs] but the combination [ty] slips to [ch] in unaccented English syllables: *picture* and *lecture* are pronounced similarly. The adverb is *fatuously* and the noun, *fatuity*, pronounced [fuh-**tyu**-uh-ti]. In this word [ty] does not become [ch] because it is in an accented syllable. (OK, if you want to keep the [ch], just use *fatuousness*.)

Fatuous refers to a kind of stupidity that is unaware of itself: "Art Major's fatuous comment that "The Thinker" was Michelangelo's best sculpture was bad enough, but he had to continue on about what a wonderful Greek sculptor Michelangelo was!" All hopes of Art learning to keep his sculptors and sculptures straight may be a fatuous dream, too.

This word is Latin fatuus "foolish, silly" in scant disguise. The Latin root *fat-* derives from the Proto-Indo-European root *bhat-*, which may also be the source of Latin battuere "to beat" and English *beat* and *bat*. If so, the original meaning of *fatuus* might have been "struck in the head." We are sure, however, that *fade* also descended from a late variant of *fatuus* via Old French *fader*. and that is something that also happens when we are battered about the head.

Filibuster • *Noun & Verb*

Pronunciation: fi-luh-bus-tur

A **filibuster** was originally a pirate, a buccaneer, a sea-faring free-booter who lived outside the law. Later this word was attached to a senator who pirates a debate by refusing to yield the floor for as long as he or she can keep talking, thereby preventing a bill from coming to a vote. Now this word refers to the activity itself.

The rules of the US Senate provide each senator with only one opportunity to speak, but no senator can be silenced unless the question is called for a vote on cloture, ending debate. A cloture vote requires a 3/5 majority (60 votes) to pass, so a filibuster succeeds so long as one senator continues to talk and 60 votes to cut off debate cannot be mustered. A person who filibusters today is a filibusterer and the activity is filibustering.

Filibuster is used apolitically in reference to verbal bullies: "The discussion was going well until Myna Bird came in and began a filibuster that squelched everyone else." Don't forget that this word does the work of a verb as well as that of a noun: "Myna filibustered the meeting until most of the attendees politely bowed out and went home."

This funny word set out as Dutch vrijbuiter "free-booter, pirate." English, however, preferred the more posh-sounding late 18th century French variant, *flibustier*, with the mysterious substitution of the L for the original R. By the mid-19th century, the word had changed to *filibuster* under the influence of Spanish filibustero "buccaneer." The point is, the word started out in English referring to the senatorial buccaneers who hijacked a debate. Later, the meaning slipped over to the process itself. Side note: The *boot* in *free-booter* is related to *booty* and the phrase "receive X to boot." This *boot* originally meant "a valuable, profit" in the days when valuables, especially smuggled valuables, were often hidden in a man's thigh-high boot.

Firkin • *Noun*

Pronunciation: fur-kin

No, a **firkin** is not a small evergreen tree but a cask or barrel, a British unit of capacity equal to half a kilderkin (= a half barrel) or a quarter of a 36-gallon barrel, or any large amount of liquid.

This lexical orphan is seldom heard these days though it is far from having outlived its usefulness. The specific meaning of this word ranges from the small to the large, from a cask you might find hanging from a St. Bernard's neck to a keg of a considerable capacity. What would a kegger be without a firkin of beer? Just be sure you spell it with an I and not a U: like the tree, not animal hair.

Why not raise the intellectual level of your next party with a promise like, "We're planning to have a firkin of fun at our party this weekend with an equal amount of beer." There are still areas of the South where from time to time people feel like saying: "Maybelle, these grits of yours are so good I could eat a firkin of them." Go ahead; try it!

This funny old word entered English from 15th century Dutch *vierdekijn* "little quarter," based on vierde "fourth, quarter" + the diminutive suffix *-kijn*. A diminutive suffix added to a noun reduces the size of the object it refers to. The Dutch suffix *-kijn* is related to both the German suffix *-chen* (as in Mädchen "girl") and English *-kin*, which survives marginally in words like *manikin* (little man) and *lambkin* (little lamb). We also find *-kin* in surnames like *Hawkins*, *Atkins*, *Tompkins*, and *Perkins*.

Flibbertigibbet • *Noun*

Pronunciation: fli-bur-dee-ji-bit

A **flibbertigibbet** is a silly, talkative scatterbrain, usually (and as usual) in reference to a woman.

You might take this word up to an adjective, *flibbertigibbetty*, but you wouldn't want to reach for the adverb, *flibbertigibbetily*, for fear your co-conversationalist might walk away before you get to the end of it. The same applies for the noun referring to the stuff flibbertigibbets are made of, *flibbertigibbetiness*: it takes much too long to utter and is fraught with potential slips of the tongue.

I think we should not allow women all the fun of this word. Male flibbertigibbets abound: "You can ask the flibbertigibbet to tell his wife when he gets home but there is little chance he will remember." For some reason flibbertigibbets are very popular on US television these days: "Denise Hurt loves to listen to the flibbertigibbets prattle on the morning and afternoon talk shows."

This is a fine word to throw out in the appropriate conversation, despite the risk of tripping over one of those syllables. The original seems to have been recorded about 1450 as fleper-gebet. It probably was a rhyming compound along the order of *yackety-yack* and *yadda-yadda-yadda*. Like these two words, it seems to have been an attempt to imitate the sound of mindless chatter, which is to say that it is onomatopoetic. Its original sense was a chatterbox or gossip, but over time it shifted to a flighty or frivolous person.

Flummox • *Verb, transitive*

Pronunciation: fluh-mucks

To **flummox** someone is to confound, bewilder, or confuse them to the point of complete frustration. This word remains a bit too slangy for formal English, so resist the temptation to use it in your senior thesis.

This funny word might have passed unnoticed in the broader English-speaking world had it not become ensconced in the vocabularies of reporters. Its spelling has fluctuated between the one you see above, *flummux*, and *flummocks*, a spelling reflected in the adjective, *flummocky* "confused, bewildered." The adjective seems to be the only derivational relative.

This word is a contribution of journalese to the general language. You find it used in newspapers like this: "The soaring stock prices of the 1990s had the experts flummoxed but didn't dampen the enthusiasm of investors." However, experts and laymen alike may be flummoxed: "Pearl was flummoxed in her search for her car keys; it never occurred to her to look in the car."

Flummox is a funny word that seems to have originated in the dialects of Gloucester, Cheshire, and Sheffield, England. In those dialects you will hear the noun flummock "slovenly person" as well as a verb to flummock "to mess up, confuse, bewilder." A closer sound match is flummocks "to maul, mangle" but, as you can see, the meaning of this word is far less compatible with that of *flummox*. We are still left with the question, where did the dialects get any of these words, a question which has etymologists, well, flummoxed.

Folderol • *Noun, mass*

Pronunciation: fawl-duh-rahl

Folderol is balderdash, blather, bunkum, claptrap, codswallop, crap, drivel, flap-doodle, garbage, gobbledygook, hogwash, horse pucky, humbug, malarkey, nonsense, piffle, poppycock, rubbish, twaddle, wish-wash, (add your favorite here). *Folderol* may also refer to a gewgaw or chachka.

English has mounted a formidable arsenal of words to stem the tide of nonsense. This funny word is one among a mighty army of synonyms mocking drivel but nothing seems to help. It is used mostly in conversation, so the spelling is a bit shaky; some prefer spelling it *falderal*. That's OK, too.

We are pretty free to substitute this funny word for any of those in its definition above: "Members of the Flat Earth Society are convinced that all this talk about a round Earth is pure folderol." Don't forget the second sense of this word though: "Lacie Curtain's place is filled with cheap folderol she collected all over the planet." By the way, ignore the rumor that they're considering changing the name of the US capital from Washington to Folderopolis—yep, just more folderol.

This word started out as a nonsense line in songs of the 19th century. Few of the songs have been recorded, since they were mostly sung from memory. Sir Walter Scott included a few lines of an old Scottish ballad in his novel *The Bride of Lammermoor* (1819): "There was a haggis in Dunbar, Fal de ral, etc., Mony better and few waur, Fal de ral, etc." In his dramatic monologue, *Mr. Sludge The Medium* (1864), Robert Browning begins a paragraph of Mr. Sludge's attempted rationalization of his (mis)deeds with "Fol-lol-the-rido-liddle-iddle-ol!" These lines are not far removed from the *fa-la-la-la-la, la-la-la* sprinkled throughout the Christmas carol, "Deck the Halls."

Formication • *Noun, mass*

Pronunciation: form-uh-**kay**-shun

No, it isn't as bad as you think: **formication** (with an M, not an N) is the appearance or skin sensation of a swarm of ants or other small bugs crawling in all directions. "Ants?!" you ask.

Yes, this word comes from the Latin verb formicare "to swarm like ants," derived from formica "ant." "*Formica* means 'ant' in Latin?" I hear disbelieving carpenters ask, "So, what about the countertop laminate of the same name? Is it made from ants?" Well, that formica—Formica® to be exact—inherited its name from an electrical insulator that, according to the official Formica® website, was a substitute for mica, which had been used up to that time. Get it? It was a replacement **for mica**. Later this material was used to make the laminate and the company decided not to change the name.

Despite the rarity of its use, this word has a remarkably large family of derivations. The immediate origin of *formication* is the verb formicate "to swarm with moving objects," as an old computer might formicate with flashing lights. The adjective, *formicant*, means "very faint or slow, crawling," as in the formicant heartbeat of someone seriously injured. If the phrase "ant farm" suggests to you that ants will germinate there in the spring, replace the phrase with the noun, *formicary*, instead. It's an English word that means the same thing.

Anything that makes your skin crawl makes you formicate: "When the teacher scraped her fingernail across the blackboard, a wave of formication spread across the classroom." If you can't think of a use for the noun, try the verb: "Holiday sales had residents formicating in the streets of New Monia all day long." This is a word guaranteed to swing the focus of attention to the speaker.

Fuddy-duddy • *Noun*

Pronunciation: fuh-dee-duh-dee

A fuddy-duddy is an old-fashioned, prudish person, an old fogy, a soft, warm milquetoast of a person who avoids anything new or exciting, but is pleasant to relax with, like an old glove. Most mama's boys grow up to be fuddy-duddies.

Fuddy-duddy itself is a fuddy-duddy of a word in that it is a bit dated, though it still retains its place in English somewhere between *milquetoast* and *square*. The plural is *fuddy-duddies*, as we saw above.

People whom this amusing word fits are generally anachronisms living at least slightly in the past: "Aunt Prudence is such an old fuddy-duddy that she would never be seen in public without a hat and gloves." Fuddy-duddies may be, however, simply people living life in the slow lane: "On the weekends the park is filled with old fuddy-duddies out for the thrill of a game of checkers."

Duddy is an old Scottish word meaning "ragged, worn out" and may well underlie *fuddy*-duddy. It is probably related to the *dud* in *duds*, a colloquial word for "clothes." In any event the implication is something comfortable but past its prime so *duds* could be behind *duddy*. So, what about *fuddy?* English-speakers love rhyme and rhythm in their language, so, as mentioned before, we find English full of rhyming compounds like *roly-poly, itsy-bitsy, dilly-dally, willy-nilly*, including the euphemism for "Jesus Christ," *jeepers-creepers*. This means that the *fuddy* in *fuddy-duddy* is pure nonsense and there is no explaining nonsense.

Furbelow • *Noun*

Pronunciation: fur-buh-lo

A **furbelow** is a flouncy ruffle on a garment, curtain, tablecloth, or the like, or indeed any attached accessory that is unnecessary but showy.

A strip of fur along the hem of an overcoat would be pretty fur far below but not necessarily a furbelow, which is a ruffle or a flounce of some sort. However, while you may flounce into a room, your dress bouncing up and down, you cannot furbelow into a room. To furbelow a room, you would have to decorate it with ruffles. Please, try to keep all these words straight.

Furbelows are generally associated with women's dress but they need not be below: "Maud Lynn Dresser wore a polka dot jumper with flowery furbelows on the shoulder straps." Still, you may occasionally see them in unexpected places, "When McDowell turned up at the fete with a furbelow on his kilt and a flounce in his walk, the womenfolk shied away from him." Of course, furbelows need not be ruffles: "Rod loves to load his car with furbelows like oversized tires, mud flaps, and running board lights."

This word is one that has seen the world. It descended from Provençal farbello "fringe," a corruption of Italian faldella, the diminutive of falda "flap, leaf, sheet." Now, falda was borrowed from a Germanic word that also gave us Old English faldan "to fold" and Modern English *fold*. The Old Germanic word also went into the compound *faldistolaz "folding stool," absorbed by Medieval Latin as faldistolium "folding chair." *Faldistolium* went on to become Old French *faldestoel* and, ultimately, Modern French fauteuil "armchair." Was that a trip or what?

Furphy • *Noun*

Pronunciation: fur-fi

A **furphy** may be a rumor, an item of gossip or scuttlebutt. It may also be a fanciful, apocryphal story.

Even though this word has a recent eponym (see below), it is already a common noun in Australia spelled with a lower case F (f). Don't forget to swap the Y for an I when you pluralize it (*furphies*). You may use the noun as a verb (I'm not furphying you) but here, too, remember the Y-I swap before endings beginning of a vowel: *furphies*, *furphied* but *furphying*. There are no other forms in wide-spread use, though we may surmise that someone who furfies a lot is a furfier.

This funny little word works as a profanity patch that helps us kick the cursing habit in sentences like this one: "No furphy, the boss and the new CFO, Lucinda Head, ran off to South America together and took most of the company's money with them." This means that the story around the office that the boss was having an affair with his secretary was—you guessed it—just another furphy.

The eponym of this funny word is an Australian businessman by the name of John Furphy, known for his famous Furphy Farm Water Carts. During the First World War these carts were converted to portable water tanks for the Australian army. The men who moved these carts from camp to camp during the war were also purveyors of rather questionable stories about the progress of the war and life at other camps. As the war progressed, the name of the water cart came to designate the gossip associated with it.

Gaberlunzie • *Noun*

Pronunciation: gæ-bur-lun-zee

A **gaberlunzie** is a strolling beggar or mendicant. In Scotland they are also sometimes called beadsmen, licensed beggars.

This word is a lexical orphan, without accompanying adjective or verb. Americans may have never encountered this word since it does not occur in any US dictionary that I know of. However, it is alive and well in Scotland, where to my surprise I recently heard it spoken.

This rather arcane yet living word refers to a wandering beggar, as opposed to one who settles down: "Candy Cain's neighborhood is still occasionally visited by a wandering gaberlunzie." However, metaphorical applications will probably be more useful: "If you lose your job when you are over 50 years old, you are likely to become a wandering gaberlunzie, begging for any position you can find."

All we know about this funny word's past is that it seems to be made up of *gaber* and *lunzie*. Now, *lunzie* is the traditional English spelling of the Scottish word lunyie "loin." The first part of the word suggests *gaberdine*, a smock or coarse cloak worn by medieval pilgrims (never made of gabardine). It is only interesting because *blue-gown* was another name for gaberlunzies in the Middle Ages—all suggestive but inconclusive. If *gaberlunzie* came from the notion of loins girded in a gaberdine, the displacement of a garment usually worn on the shoulders needs an explanation. I have none.

Gardyloo! • *Interjection*

Pronunciation: gahr-di-**loo**

Contrary to popular belief, the colorful expression **gardyloo** does not mean "protect the bathroom"; rather, it is an exclamatory warning alerting passers-by to dirty water or worse about to be dropped from a window above.

The second-floor dwellers in obscure parts of Scotland traditionally shout this warning before emptying their wash bowls and slop buckets onto the street below. It is a good word to know when strolling the by-ways of Kiltland even if it is of little use elsewhere.

Since the invention of indoor plumbing, the need for this interjection has contracted considerably. Moreover, since it is an interjection, it is used alone and not in sentences, making the creation of example sentences problematic. However, if you think dropping water bombs from upper-story windows will help cooler heads prevail in the world below, you might cover your actions by shouting, "Gardyloo!" before loosing your next aquagrenade.

Legend has it that French King Philippe Auguste (1180-1223) was drenched with the contents of a chamber pot while strolling the streets of Paris one afternoon. His reaction to this misfortune was to issue an edict directing all Parisians to exclaim, *gare à l'eau!* "look out for the water" before dumping sordid liquids from an upper-story window. While France eventually forgot this courtesy, the Scots took it more to heart, adding the magic of Scots English to the sophisticated French phrase, thereby creating this funny little exclamation. Or so the legend goes.

Gastromancy • *Noun, mass*

Pronunciation: gæs-truh-mæn-si

Telling someone's fortune from their stomach rumblings was a giant leap forward from the earlier use of animal entrails for the same purpose. Both types of divination have been referred to as **gastromancy**. Gastromancy can also be fortune-telling using a clear pot-bellied glass bowl filled with water placed in front of candles, a forerunner of crystal-ball gazing.

Did you ever wonder what people did before television? This word names a popular 17th century pastime that declined in the 18th century with the discovery that practitioners of gastromancy were using ventriloquism (gastriloquism?) to manufacture stomach sounds similar to words. The adjective and agent noun is *gastromantic*.

Tired of watching TV after dinner? Then just remain at the table and introduce gastromancy with an off-hand comment like: "I just adored the cabbage, black beans, and sausage, Frederica. Now, let's see what we can predict of tomorrow's weather by gastromancy." Should we not want to play this game, at least we have a more sophisticated term for stomach-rumblings, "After all that beer, George, your stomach is erupting in a gastromantic chorus. From it I predict you are in for a long night of heart-burn and a headache in the morning."

This funny little word is the English version of Greek gastromanteia "divination by the belly" made up of gaster "pot-belly" + mant-eia "power of divination." *Gaster* may be related to English *graze* and that which is grazed upon, *grass*, though the connection is shaky. *Manteia*, however, is related to Latin mens, mentis "mind, soul, feelings," found in English *mental* and the noun suffix *-ment*. Sanskrit mantar "thinker" and Russian mudryi (from older *mond-rii*) "wise" are also relatives.

Gazump • *Verb, transitive*

Pronunciation: guh-**zump**

To **gazump** is to sell a house to a higher bidder after accepting a lower bid from someone else or to raise the price just before signing the contract. Today its meaning has expanded to cover just about any kind of irregular trumping to gain something by questionable means.

This ostensibly Yiddish word has a surprisingly normal family. The participle, *gazumping*, may be used as an adjective and action noun: "Norman is known for his gazumping more than any other real estate agent in town." The person who gazumps is known, unsurprisingly, as a gazumper.

Laws in the US prevent real estate gazumping but elsewhere in the English-speaking world it still sometimes rears its amusing if ugly head: "If you're buying a house in that neighborhood, sign the contract as soon as possible, before you are gazumped." Anyone may use this word in its second sense, however, to unfairly trump someone: "I had the committee convinced we should pave the parking lot but the boss gazumped my suggestion with a proposal to increase bonuses this year."

Someone has suggested that this word may have been borrowed from a Yiddish verb gazumpn "to overcharge," but I have not been able to verify the existence of such a word. *Gazump* first popped up in the 1920s in England and was used in the sense of swindling someone by overcharging. However, the word was not widely used until the real estate boom in the 1970s. London in the 1970s was a place and time of rapidly rising real estate prices—perfect conditions for gazumping by double selling houses and apartments. It was at that time that the word picked up the meaning usually associated with it these days.

Gobbledygook • *Noun, mass*

Pronunciation: gah-bul-dee-gook

This silly slang word refers to pretentious bureaucratic jargon; the complicated language of red tape, bureaucratese.

Gobbledygook is a loner; it has no adjective or verb, not even a plural. Of course, it is not standard or formal English so only use it humorously in (very) informal conversations. Never sign a legal document containing this word or what it refers to.

The creator of this word originally intended it as a more descriptive terms for bureaucratese: "I can't read all that gobbledygook on the tax returns; I sent the IRS what I could afford and left it up to them to fill out the forms." However, it is the stock and trade of any con artist who tries to pretext you: "The guy fed me some gobbledygook about a banking investigation that required a check for $2000 from me, so I threw him out."

Texas cattleman Samuel Maverick (1803-1870) not only gave English its word *maverick* (see page 78), he also gave us his grandson, Maury Maverick. Maury served two terms in the US House of Representatives (1935-1939), where he had difficulty communicating with his congressional colleagues. He said it was because they spoke gobbledygook. When asked what that was, he responded that the word was based on the sound turkeys (the flying kind) made back home in Texas. They are "...always gobbledy-gobbling and strutting with ludicrous pomposity." At the end of this gobble, according to Representative Maverick, there is a sort of "gook."

CR

Gobemouche · *Noun*

Pronunciation: go-buh-moosh

A **gobemouche** is a highly credulous naif, a very gullible person who believes everything he or she hears no matter how absurd.

Admittedly, this funny little word is not a common, ordinary word that you hear around the house every day. It is interesting, though, for its etymology and the decoration it adds to any conversation. Since it is so rarely used, it has remained a lexical orphan without producing any related words.

In the US, the metaphors for gullibility are buying swampland in Florida, desert land in Arizona and, if you want to go back to the 50s, the Brooklyn Bridge: "If you are such a gobemouche as to believe that I am a rocket scientist, you might be interested in buying my share of the Brooklyn Bridge." Wherever you find gullibility, look for gobemouches: "What kind of gobemouche would think that we can tow icebergs from the Arctic Circle to the Sahara Desert for irrigation?"

This word is a French compound noun based on gober "to swallow" + mouche "fly," literally, a fly-swallower. The image here is someone whose jaw drops upon hearing a fantastic story too good to be true. *Gober* is suspected of being borrowed from Celtic, though no one knows for sure. For sure it was later borrowed back into English as *gobble*—not the turkey noise but the impolite eating style. *Mouche* is the French remnant of Latin musca "fly," which shares its origins with Russian mukha "fly." It also evolved into Spanish mosca "fly" with its diminutive, mosquito "little fly." Well, you know what English did with that one.

Godwottery • *Noun, mass*

Pronunciation: gahd-**wah**-duh-ree

Godwottery can be several things: an exaggeratedly romantic, highly elaborate garden, usually composed of bizarrely incompatible plants and objects d'art. It can also refer to a love or affection for such gardens or even affected, archaic language.

This word is a sort of marginal piece of verbal godwottery itself. It comes as no surprise that such an eccentric word has no direct relations—not even a plural. It is a fish out of the current conversational waters so, if we don't return it to its natural habitat, it will soon no longer be with us.

You are always safe using this word in reference to gardens: "Rose Bush's backyard is a godwottery of every kind of plant crawling over gnomes, flamingos, gates without fences, and several sets of garden furniture." As for language, I still consider it wise to add a qualifier to make the reference to language clear: "Noah Zarq speaks in such verbal godwottery only a Shakespearean scholar could understand him."

This funny word originated as a phrase from the line, 'A garden is a lovesome thing, God wot!' in T. E. Brown's poem *My Garden* (1876). *Wot* is a variant of the verb *wit*, from Old English witan "to know," so the phrase originally meant "God knows," which obviously has nothing to do with gardening. Both our words *wit* and *wisdom* are derivations from the Old English verb. It is a cousin to German wissen "know," and distantly related to Polish wiedziec "to know" and Russian vesti "news."

Gongoozle • *Verb, transitive*

Pronunciation: gahng-**goo**-zul

Gongoozle means to ogle, to rubber-neck, gawk at, to go goo-goo eyed over, to simply stare intensely at something like a gobemouche.

This funny word has been around since the turn of the century but gained currency in the 1970s among Britain's canal travelers. Gongoozlers are those who gongoozle, of course, and their occupation is known up and down the canals as gongoozling.

I see no reason for quarantining this dandy expression to the British canal system. Do bring it up from time to time as friends drop by: "Don't just stand around gongoozling: grab a paintbrush and join in the fun!" And why not call the gongoozlers at football games what they are? *Spectator* has much too staid a ring about it. But then if you are away at college, you know that guys gongoozling gals and vice versa is a sporting event itself (and forget the phrase *scoping out*).

The origin of this word is uncertain but it may have originated in Lincolnshire, England as a combination of gawn "to stare vacantly or curiously" + gooze "to stare aimlessly, gape." It is conceivably related to the word goozle "throat" or "uvula," that little punching bag hanging from the top of the back of your throat. It is visible when the mouth is agape, as it is during very serious gongoozling. *Goozle* originated in Scotland meaning "throat" and might have influenced the originator of this word. The similarity of this funny word to *ogle*, *goo-goo eyes*, and *goggles* is probably not an innocent one, either.

Gonzo • *Adjective & Noun*

Pronunciation: gahn-zo

Gonzo means bizarre, outrageously unusual, 'far out.'

This odd term first appeared in a 1971 article by William Cardoza of the *Boston Globe* in reference to journalist-novelist Hunter Thompson, author of the novel *Fear and Loathing in Las Vegas*. Thompson was a journalist who seemed out of control. His bizarre off-center reportage of the Kentucky Derby focused on the drugs, sex, and vulgar behavior of the attendees rather than the race at the center of other reporters' attention.

Gonzo is still an adjective skulking in the shadows of English, not yet fully outted except as the name of the purple Muppet on the children's TV show, *Sesame Street* (Gonzo the Great). In colloquial US English, however, you hear it occasionally in phrases like this: "Sally Forth showed up at the party in a gonzo outfit that looked like something she picked up at a second-hand clothing store in the sixties."

Cardoza claimed that *gonzo* came from Boston slang, which means it probably originated from Italian gonzo "idiot, fool." This word goes back to the Proto-Indo-European root ghans- "goose," which became German Gans "goose" and English *gander*, extended by the ever-popular -*er* suffix. The association of geese with dimwits is common in Indo-European languages, as we see in the English expression, "you silly goose." This sense became the dominant one in Italian and today it is the only meaning of *gonzo* ("goose" is *oca*). The sense of "outlandish" in Boston slang could have resulted from the misprision of the Italian word by the Irish-Catholics of Boston.

Goombah • *Noun*

Pronunciation: goom-bah

Goombah is Italian-American slang for a godfather, patron, mentor. It could also indicate a friend or associate, or a even a buddy, especially one in a position to help you.

Goombah is used mostly by Americans of Italian ancestry in referring to each other. Calling someone who is not Italian *goombah* sounds a bit odd, unless you are Italian yourself. It is a slang term, though, so use it carefully whatever your ancestry.

This word refers to an influential friend who looks out for your interests and helps you when the need arises, "Mario has a goombah in city hall who takes care of all his parking tickets." *Goombah* also assumes a meaning not far removed from that of *sugar daddy*: "I'm not going to buy you a car just because you managed to get a driver's license. Look, I'm your father, not your goombah."

This funny word probably comes from cumbare "respected older man, godfather" a word from a southern Italian dialect. Such a word would be a descendant of Medieval Latin compater "co-priest, godfather." We have written evidence of such a word in Old French compeer "an equal, a friend." The Latin word is a combination of com- "(together) with" + pater "father." *Pater* went on to become *padre* in Spanish and Italian, and *père* in French. The same root underlying *pater* came directly from Proto-Indo-European through Old Germanic to German as *Vater* and to English as *father*.

Hemidemisemiquaver • *Noun*

Pronunciation: he-mi-de-mi-**se**-mi-kway-vur

A **hemidemisemiquaver** is a term in classical British musical terminology meaning a four-flagged musical note played for 1/64 the duration of a whole note. It lasts half as long as a thirty-second note (or demisemiquaver) and a quarter as long as a sixteenth note (semiquaver). A second meaning of this giant among words is, ironically enough, an almost infinitesimally small amount.

This word is the kind of word musicians think up as they sit around discussing music and drinking late at night. I chose this word because it oddly reflects all the variants of the borrowed English prefixes for "half": *hemi-*, *demi-*, and *semi-*. I thought you might like to know why we have three of these little critters.

This long word might seem to be joined at the hip to the music world: "Moseley, I think you are pausing a hemidemisemiquaver at the beginning of each bar, which puts you noticeably behind the other members of the orchestra by the end of the piece." However, the idea behind the word has caught on enough in England that *hemidemisemi-* is now a prefix referring to things exceptionally small: "I don't think that Germaine has so much as a hemidemisemi-idea of what this project is all about."

The bizarre load of prefixes meaning "half" at the beginning of this word reflects our borrowing variants of the same original word from several languages. *Hemi-* is a Greek form meaning "half." *Semi-* is the Latin version derived from the same Proto-Indo-European root. *Demi-* is an Old French reduction of Latin dimidius "split in two," made up of dis- "apart" + medius "half." English, of course, could not resist the temptation to help itself to them all.

Hobbledehoy • *Noun*

Pronunciation: hah-bul-di-hoy

A **hobbledehoy** is an awkward, bad-mannered young boy, in particular one struggling to come to grips with adulthood.

Obviously, this funny word was created to have fun with and the English writers have well met that expectation. Thackeray referred to this awkward stage of boyhood as *hobbledehoyhood* and Trollope called it *hobbledehoydom*. Those who behave like a hobbledehoy have been called *hobbledhoyish*, a reflection of their *hobbledhoyism*.

Why litter your speech with such short slang words as *geek* and *nerd* when you have this ripplingly long noun at your disposal: "I remember dating some hobbledehoy in high school who thought Chardonnay was a French actress!" This word trips across our tongues so pleasantly that we should use it for sheer delight of the experience: "Hey, Sis! Some gum-smacking hobbledehoy on a motorcycle says he's here to pick you up!"

No one has any idea where this word came from but this fact never impeded a true word nerd. This word has assumed so many forms since its emergence in the 16th century that it would be difficult to track them all backwards: *hobbard de hoy, hobberdy-hoy, habberdehoy, hobby de hoy, hobidehoy, ho-body hoy*, or *hobberdehoy*. Its current shape associates it with *hobble*, an awkward or clumsy gait, and *hoy*, an awkward and clumsy person, a word that was lost somewhere in the hustle if not the bustle of the 17th century. So the most likely origin is the phrase *hobble hoy*, which very few people could spell correctly over history.

CR

Hocus-pocus • *Noun, mass*

Pronunciation: ho-kus po-kus]

Hocus-pocus is a "magic" word uttered by a magician that is supposed to call forth the magic of a prestidigitator; it is a near synonym of *abracadabra*. It may, however, be used in reference to magic tricks themselves or, metaphorically, any trickery involving behind-the-scenes or under-the-table deception.

Since this word is a noun, given the English tendency to 'verb' nouns freely, you will probably run into words like *hocus-pocused* and *hocus-pocusing*. *Hocus-pokery* doesn't surprise me at all, given the potential influence of *jiggery-pokery* with the same meaning.

Hocus-pocus began its life as a phrase uttered by magicians imitating the magic words used by witches to cast spells: "You want a raise in your allowance? Do you think I can say, 'Hocus-pocus,' and pull money out of my ear?" However, since magicians depend on a kind of deception, today this word most often refers to real trickery: "What sort of hocus-pocus did Phil Anders use to get Marian Kine to go out with him?"

In his book on witchcraft, *A Candle in the Dark* (1655), Thomas Ady wrote: "I will speak of one man...that went about in King James his time...who called himself, The Kings Majesties most excellent Hocus Pocus, and so was called, because that at the playing of every Trick, he used to say, Hocus pocus, tontus talontus, vade celeriter jubeo, a dark composure of words, to blinde the eyes of the beholders, to make his Trick pass the more currently without discovery." Archbishop John Tillotson later claimed in 1742, "In all probability those common juggling words of *hocus pocus* are nothing else but a corruption of *hoc est corpus*, by way of ridiculous imitation of the priests of the Church of Rome in their trick of Transubstantiation."

Hoosegow • *Noun*

Pronunciation: hoos-gæw

A **hoosegow** is a slang word for a jail or prison.

This word is a facetious slang word rarely found in formal English. The S is more usually pronounced [z] but the preferred pronunciation is with an [s]. The plural of *hoosegow* is *hoosegows* and that is the only form or family it has.

Although this word may be used to refer to prisons, it most often indicates the local jail (that's *gaol*, if you live outside the US): "Miss Deeds collected parking tickets for 12 years and refused to pay them until threatened with a weekend in the hoosegow." Always expect to get a smile when you say something like this: "Bud Light has boozed his way into the local hoosegow so many times, he is more at home there than he is at home."

This word is a mispronunciation of the Spanish word, juzgado [huz-**gah**-dho] "a court, tribunal," that was borrowed out West. The Spanish word is based on the verb juzgar "to judge," the Spanish descendant of Latin iudicare "to pass judgment." The Latin word goes back to the noun, ius [yus] "law." Since Classical Latin didn't have the letters J or Y, the Romans used the letter I the way we use Y: as a consonant before vowels (as in *yes*) and as a vowel after consonants (as in *very*). Later Romance languages, such as French, Italian, and Spanish, replaced the consonantal I with J. For that reason the root *ius* is written with a J in many English words borrowed from Romance languages, such as *just*, *justice*, and *judge*.

Hootenanny • *Noun*

Pronunciation: hoot-næ-nee

Hootenanny started its life meaning a thingamabob, thingamajig, or whatchamacallit. From there it was but a hop and a skip to mean something insignificant. Now it refers to a folk or country music jam session.

The *Oxford English Dictionary*, known to collect every word that has ever appeared in English print, gives three spellings of this word: *hootnanny*, *hootenanny*, and *hootananny*. Those who use this word seem to have settled on the one above.

We probably owe this word's sense of "a folksong session" to Pete Seeger, who popularized it in the 30s: "Y'all bring your guitars when you come tonight and we'll have a good ol' timey hootenanny." Among older Southerners, you still hear this word used to refer to a thingamabob: "Well, I got the lawnmower back together but I have this little hootenanny here left over. Do you know what it's for?"

No one seems to know where this word came from, which unfetters us to speculate. The word first appeared at the beginning of the 20th century in the sense of "doohickey, thingamabob." For the third meaning, I would bet on an old Southern expression, *hoot 'na holler* "a hoot and a holler," used now to refer to a small distance: "They live just a hoot 'na holler from here." However, my grandparents often referred to children making a lot of noise as "a-hootin' an' a-hollerin'." The interesting connection here is that the *-in' an'* reduces to the *enan* we find in the middle of *hootenanny*. It is imaginable that the *hollerin'* was dropped, leaving *hootin' an'*. All we then need is the common English suffix, *-y* to give us *hootenanny*.

Jackanapes • *Noun*

Pronunciation: jæ-kuh-nayps

A **jackanapes** can be a domesticated ape or monkey or a human knave, rogue, or blackguard. Most often it is used to refer to an annoyingly impudent and, usually, young person.

Given the rich variety of insults with which the English language presents us, it is a shame that our preference tends more and more to common vulgarities. This word is an excellent substitute for some of the commoner insults and deserves a more exalted place in our insult inventory. Jackanapes are always up to no-good jackanapery when they behave jackanapishly. The plural of this noun is simple: *jackanapes*, too.

Please help stamp out the simple-minded four-letter insults we are swimming in by saying things like this: "Jack is the jackanapes who busted our jack-o'-lantern last Halloween." Unfortunately, jackanapes themselves abound: "Lending policies of the jackanapes on Wall Street brought the world economic system to its knees just after the turn of the century." Now, isn't that more civil than what most people call them?

This word came from a derisive nickname for William de la Pole, the first Duke of Suffolk, murdered in 1450. He was called "Jack Napes" because a block and chain similar to those used on trained monkeys of the time were on his family coat of arms. In those days *Jack* was slang for "man," similar to *guy* or *dude* today. We still see it in such phrases as "jack-in-the-box," "every man Jack of them," and a particular favorite of October's, "jack-o'-lantern." The origin of the A and N are still in dispute. The A probably came from a reduction of the preposition *of,* as we see in *jack-o'-lantern* and *will-o'-the-wisp.* Since this reduction must precede a consonant, not a vowel, the N may well have been added fortuitously in response to that demand.

Kerfuffle • *Noun*

Pronunciation: kur-**fuh**-ful

A **kerfuffle** is an uproar, an agitation, a fuss or brouhaha (see page 21), a commotion that produces ruffled feathers.

This lexical odd-ball comes from the land that specializes in odd-ball words, Scotland. Since it is spoken more than written, no one really knows how it is spelled: *carfuffle*, *curfuffle*, or several other alternatives proffered over the years, with and without the R. The Australians have added *kerfoofle*, *kafuffle*, and *kafoofle*. *Kerfuffle* is the best way to spell this word today. Trust me.

If you need to bring a true brouhaha under control, the question "What is all the *kerfuffle* about?" is much more likely to gain the desired results than "What is all the fuss about?" Those involved will have to belay the kerfuffle to look this word up in the dictionary. It is a lovely word for all its quirks. "I hear she raised a big *kerfuffle* over the alimony," soothes the ear where all the alternatives grate.

The older spelling of this word, *carfuffle*, suggests the first syllable may have originated in Gaelic car "twist, bend, turn about," the same meaning as the Scottish verb *fuffle* that follows it. The spelling *kerfuffle*, on the other hand, suggests that the prefix may be *ker-*, found in such interjections as *kerplop* and *kersplash*. We aren't sure of either source. Nor is there any reliable clue as to where *fuffle* originated. It has been intimated to be a blend of *fuss* and *shuffle*. Since blends are rare, however, we must concede at this point that no one really knows—or they're keeping it to themselves.

Klutz • *Noun*

Pronunciation: kluts

A **klutz** is a dolt, a jerk, a putz, a schlemiel, which is to say, a clumsy, awkward person who seldom gets anything right.

Klutziness is the abstract noun that pinpoints the klutz's problem. As you can see in the definition above, it is enough of a problem that we have joined forces with Yiddish to create a sufficiency of words to express it. The noun allows the adjective *klutzy* (*klutzier*, *klutziest*). Don't forget to add E when you write the plural, *klutzes*.

The fun in this word is that it is almost onomatopoetic: it just sounds right for its meaning: "M. T. Head is such a klutz that he tied his shoes together and fell on the dog when he tried to stand up." That example gives you some idea of what defines a klutz. "In the middle of summer that klutz, Lucinda Head, left a dozen chocolate bars on top of her dashboard—which is now chocolate coated."

This word is another gift from Yiddish, this time klots "block, log," borrowed from German *Klotz* with the same meaning. The semantic connection here parallels that of our own *blockhead*, which originally referred to a wooden block on which hats are shaped. The same root behind the German word turned up in English as both *clot* and *clod*. This word is historically unrelated to the *Klux* in *Ku Klux Klan*. This organization is not the Ku Klutz Klan, as some mispronounce it, though the misperception is understandable.

La-di-da • *Interjection*

Pronunciation: lah-dee-dah

La-di-da is an interjection used to deride the supercilious and pompous. It is an appropriate introduction to any comment on someone affecting superiority; flaunting their wealth or otherwise acting haughty or disdainful.

Most speakers stick with using this word as a derisive interjection, especially when we see something showy: "Well, la-di-da, aren't we all dressed up for the occasion?" But, as we will see below, others exploit it more broadly.

Although this word is used by far most widely as an interjection, because it is a bit of silliness, we do not hesitate to use it as a noun, adjective, or verb when it pleases us: "Phil Anders found some la-di-da heiress in New York and left Lucy Lastik for her!" If you feel you must write such expressions, remember to always add an apostrophe before -s (*la-di-da's*) and an H before other suffixes: "Fowler Fairweather la-di-dahed his way through Ha-a-avard but the job on Wall Street has reduced his hat by a size or two."

Some of you might remember the 1940s when *swell* was a slang adjective meaning "great, just fine." Well, *swell* was originally a derogatory term of the 18th century that referred to those pompous members of the upper class who puffed themselves up, acting superior to others. Since lard at the time was one of the main causes of human swelling, a rhyming compound, *lardy-dardy*, created on the model of *roly-poly*, *helter-skelter*, and *dilly-dally*, emerged in British slang. The British reluctance to pronounce Rs at the end of syllables quickly led to the word we have today: *la-di-da*.

Lagopodous • *Adjective*

Pronunciation: lu-**gah**-puh-dus

Lagopodous means rabbit-footed, having feet like a rabbit, or having feet thickly covered with fur or feathers, like the Alpine ptarmigan.

Here is a word you might think peripheral enough to omit from your vocabulary. However, it has a slightly more specific meaning than mere *rabbit-footed*, a word I am sure you find great use for. A creature with feet like a rabbit is a lagopus—and probably a sourpuss, too, if he isn't a rabbit. *Lagopodously* would describe doing something in a floppy-footed manner.

I know what you are thinking: why would any normal human being need this word? But I was frustrated for years at the lack of a word to describe my aunt, who loved flopping lagopodously around the house in her bunny slippers. If you look around, you'll find places where it plays well, too: "Jerry Attrick looks like a lagopodous leprechaun, lunging through the snow in his green hat, outdated ski suit, and oversized snowshoes."

This word is made up of Greek lagos "rabbit" + pous (pod-) "foot." *Lagos* is a distant relation of English *slack*, sharing a common ancestor (s)log- "slack, loose." This ancient word had a Fickle S that often fell off in the process of historical development, hence Latin laxus "slack, loose" but English *slack*, both of which derive from *(s)log-*. The semantic connection between the sense of slackness and bunnies lies less in their feet than in those lax, slack, floppy ears on their heads.

Lickety-split • *Adverb*

Pronunciation: li-ki-ti-split

Moving **lickety-split** is moving extremely fast or quickly. This word is an adverb that tells us how some activity is carried out.

Lickety-split has a substantial if rather queer family of relatives. To cut quickly across the lawn is to run lickety-cut, fast horses run lickety-click on a hard surface, and a car might go lickety-smash into a tree if the driver were not careful. *Lickety* is used almost as a prefix in English, though we tend to hear it mostly in *lickety-split*.

Any sudden, fast motion qualifies for lickety-split: "William Arami leapt from his chair and ran lickety-split down the hall when he saw Marian Kine pass by." However, the motion need not be pedestrian or vehicular: "Imogene, would you write up an innocent explanation of our CEO's arrest and get it out over the wires lickety-split? Thanks."

The first component of this funny word comes from a slang use of the word *lick* meaning to run or move very fast: "Harley's wheels licked down the road like a bolt of lightning." When combined with other verbs, however, it not only converts them to adverbs but extends itself to *lickety*. This is probably the result of adding the common suffix -*y* to the phrase *lick it*, as to lick it out of the massage parlor as fast as you can. *Lick* itself has relatives throughout the Indo-European languages, with and without the Fickle N often found in Latin but not in Germanic languages. In Latin we find lingere "to lick" and lingua "tongue," which led to *language* and *linguistics*, both borrowed from French. English also borrowed *lecher* from French, a word related in ways I need not explain.

Lickspittle • *Noun*

Pronunciation: lik-spit-ul

A **lickspittle** is a fawning toady, a sycophant, a bootlick, a yes-man, or a brown-noser.

Here is a synonym of *toady* that takes a little longer to pronounce but is more of an attention-grabber. For those of you whose imaginations and stomachs find this word difficult, *toady* is always there. If you like to be noticed, though, this word will work better for you.

Lickspittles are found high and low: "The corporate lickspittles in Washington often introduce bills in Congress written by lobbyists." They also turn up at home, in the workplace, and all around the neighborhood: "The president's idea of putting a solar powered flashlight into production ASAP was supported by all the toadies and lickspittles in upper management, so we are going to do it."

This rather repulsive word is a combination of the verb *lick* and the noun *spittle*, derived from the verb *spit*. The word refers to someone who so fawns over you that they are willing to lick up your spit. (Excuse me, but it's true.) Both are veteran English words, unborrowed and untainted by outside influence. As mentioned on the previous page, *Lick* is a variant of a Proto-Indo-European stem that turns up in most Indo-European languages in the expected local form: Latin *lingere*, Greek *leikhein*, and Russian *lizat'*. *Lick* may be of imitative origin (onomatopoetic): Hebrew *likek* and Arabic *laqqa* "licked" are historically unrelated to the English word though they sound suspiciously similar. The best explanation is that all these words are onomatopoetic sound imitations.

Logorrhea • *Noun, mass*

Pronunciation: lah-guh-**ree**-uh

Logorrhea is excessively wordy, incoherent speech, a storm of gibberish, possibly the result of mental instability.

Although this word means about the same as 'excessive wordiness,' its rhyme with *diarrhea* adds to it a pejorative vividness. In fact, the phrase *verbal diarrhea* is often used when this word would be more discreet and impressive. Remember to double the R in this and all other words with this root referring to a flow. Outside the US you are allowed to spell this word *logorrhoea*. You have your choice of adjectives: *logorrheal* or *logorrhetic*.

When *wordiness* just isn't quite enough, this word is what you need: "When Donny Brooke saw his daughter's new eyebrow rings with matching lip rings, he went from silence to sputtering logorrhea in fewer than five seconds." Notice the pejorative implication here: Donny was not uttering flattering niceties. Radio and TV run on logorrhea: "Lacie McBride seems to enjoy the ceaseless logorrhea of the talk shows on radio and TV."

This word is a compound made up of Greek logos "word, idea" + rhe-in "to flow, run." *Logos* goes back to a Proto-Indo-European root *log-/leg-* (see *ablaut* in the glossary) that is also behind the roots of *lexical* (*lex* = *leg-s-*), as well as *legislate* and *legal*. The semantic connection between the senses of "word" and "law" apparently comes from an era when the word of the king was the law. Greek rhein "to flow" comes from the root *sreu-*, which originally began with a Fickle S that was lost in Greek. In the Germanic languages, however, the S remained and picked up a T producing German *Strom* and English *stream*.

Lollygag • *Verb, intransitive*

Pronunciation: lah-li-gæg

Lollygag has two meanings. The first is humorous slang meaning to dawdle, to mess around, to delay someone or something by moving slowly. The second is to mess around in the sense of petting or necking in secret, away from prying eyes.

Remember to double up on the Gs when you add a suffix to this silly word: *lollygagged, lollygagging, lollygagger. Lollygagging* serves as both an adjective and process noun, so you can speak freely of someone's lollygagging or their lollygagging ways.

You wouldn't want to use such a substandard slang word like *lollygag* in a job application, but it is a funny word to use when you want to hurry someone up without offending them: "Griselda, stop lollygagging and let's go. You can put your nails on when we get back!" This lets Griselda know that you are still in a good mood. Be careful not to confuse the second sense of this word with the first, though: "Griselda, I heard that you and Les Canoodle were lollygagging in the back of his car last Saturday night." In Britain, where lolly is loot from a crime and gagging is choking, this quaint Americanism might evoke less amusement.

This word is compounded from loll "to lie about, relax" + gag "to trick, fool." *Loll* is still used in phrases such as loll about "to do nothing, take it easy." The verb *to gag*, however, isn't used today in the sense of "to fool," but the noun *gag* is still lolling around with the meaning "a joke or trick." The original compound seems to have implied a delay amounting to tomfoolery. A bit of that meaning lingers in the canoodling sense of *lollygag* today.

Malarkey • *Noun, mass*

Pronunciation: muh-**lahr**-kee

Malarkey means balderdash, blather, bunkum, claptrap, crap, drivel, garbage, horse pucky, humbug, nonsense, piffle, poppycock, rigmarole, rubbish, twaddle.

Judging from the long but still partial list of synonyms in the definition above, it would seem that English speakers have a low tolerance for speech that doesn't make sense (see also *codswallop* on page 29 and *folderol* on page 48). We go out of our way to create nonsensical words to express the notion of nonsense. Well, at least that makes sense.

Although it is a good English word, this one is another you wouldn't use in formal writing. It is strictly for conversational purposes: "There is more malarkey in the philosophy department here than there is on Capitol Hill." It is true that malarkey surrounds us: "I haven't heard so much malarkey since Phil Anders tried to explain what he and his research assistant were up to in the cloak room."

This word first emerged in the US in 1922 but no one knows where it came from. There is an Irish surname, Malarkey, but no one of that name seems to have been blessed with a greater gift of blarney than any other Irishman. Someone has suggested that it might be related to Greek malakos "soft," but *malarkey* doesn't seem to be the concoction of someone versed in the classics. We will have to chalk it up as another mystery unsolved by the word sleuths. And that's no malarkey.

Maverick • *Noun*

Pronunciation: mæ-vrik

A **maverick** is a calf or other animal that has left the herd and has not been branded, so that anyone who brands it can claim ownership. It can also be a garrulous individualist, an iconoclast who lives by his or her own rules, posing some kind of threat to others.

Maverick is rather a maverick of a word, a garrulous individual with no lexical kin. It may, however, be used 'as is' adjectivally, "Buck Shott is a maverick CEO who took a chance when no one else would to produce pedal-powered wheelchairs."

Although we generally use this word to refer to iconoclasts who pose some sort of threat, we owe a lot to mavericks. Charles Darwin and Galileo were among the scientific mavericks who grandly expanded our understanding of the world and the universe. Henry Ford started out as a maverick who revolutionized manufacturing. Those of us who have been around for a while remember Bret (James Garner) and Bart (Jack Kelly) Maverick on the US TV show *Maverick*, popular in the 1960's. They were cowboys who lived around the edge of the law, mavericks among the TV cowboy heroes of the time in their fecklessness.

The eponym of this word is Texas cattleman Samuel Maverick (1803-1870), who let the calves in his herd roam unbranded. Initially ranchers, who 'adopted' them, simply referred to them as "Maverick's" but the term soon migrated into *mavericks*. An interesting side note: Sam's grandson, Maury Maverick, coined the word *gobbledygook* to describe bureaucratic doubletalk while serving in the U.S. Congress (see page 57 for the details).

ભ

Mollycoddle • *Verb, transitive*

Pronunciation: mah-li-kah-dul

Mollycoddle means to pamper, to coddle, to treat someone in an overly protective way, as you would a child. In some regions it also means an effeminate man or boy.

Which is preferable: to overindulge, to spoil, to pamper, to coddle, or mollycoddle someone? *To pamper* someone is to give them everything they want, especially luxury items. *To overindulge* means to allow them to have their way more than is advisable. *To spoil* means to pamper someone to the point that it harms their character, while *to coddle* or *mollycoddle* means to treat someone as a child, to overprotect them.

Here is a playful word that you can use liberally around the house: "Stop mollycoddling that son of yours and make him do some housework this weekend." I hope she doesn't turn around and say, "Should I stop mollycoddling you and expect the same from you?" Don't leave the noun *mollycoddle* behind: "I like Curly Hair but I'm not sure a mollycoddle like him would help our rugby team much."

This funny word is actually a compound noun based on molly "an effeminate man" plus coddle "to undercook; to be slack on discipline." *Molly* was originally a nickname for *Mary* but, like the nickname for *John*, *Jack*, it soon took on a life of its own. Applying *Molly* to a man implies femininity, just as does the diminutive of *sister*, *sissy*. *Coddle* means "cook an egg in water without boiling it," hence undercooking it. From this sense of undercooking to underdoing discipline is but a very short hop.

Mugwump • *Noun*

Pronunciation: mug-wump

Capitalized, **Mugwump** refers to a Republican who refused to support the party's presidential candidate, James G. Blaine, in 1884. Uncapitalized, **mugwump** refers to a person who cannot make up his or her mind, a person who switches positions or takes no position on an issue. According to US folklore, a mugwump is a bird with its mug on one side of the fence and his wump on the other.

This word comes from a jovial family of words, including the nouns *mugwumpism*, if you prefer formality, or *mugwumpery*, if not. People who behave like mugwumps are mugwumpish and behave mugwumpishly.

The disadvantage of being an independent in the US is that independents have no interesting name associated with them: we call them simply "independents." Well, here is the word to pull independents off that snag: "With the Democrats and Republicans almost evenly divided this year, the mugwumps are likely to decide the outcome of the presidential election."

Republicans borrowed this word from the original Americans, in this case from Massachusett, an Algonquian language originally spoken in the state named after the people who spoke it. In 1663, the Reverend John Eliot of Roxborough, Massachusetts, published the first grammar of the language. According to Eliot, the Massachusetts called their chief a mugquomp. Although the first published example of this word appeared only in 1828, there is ample reason to believe that it was used earlier as a facetious term referring to American leaders from Europe. When the Europeans adopted it, they retained the sarcasm.

CR

Mumpsimus • *Noun*

Pronunciation: mump-suh-mus

A **mumpsimus** is an old-fashioned person who obstinately clings to traditional ways and notions despite evidence that they are wrong or harmful, or the old-fashioned notions themselves.

I know what you are thinking: this must be a mistake, *mumpsimus* has to be the medical term for someone with mumps. Not at all; the similarity is pure happenchance. This is another funny word that resulted from a mispronunciation which, because of the peculiarity of its circumstances, stuck in the language.

A mumpsimus is a curmudgeon firmly stuck in the mud of time: "Andy Bellam is an incorrigible mumpsimus who still writes letters on his old Smith-Corona typewriter." Keep in mind that a mumpsimus may also be the out-dated notion that a mumpsimus clings to: "Andy still holds firmly to the old mumpsimus that walking beneath a ladder brings bad luck."

Mumpsimus is a lexical peculiarity better explained with a story than a formal etymology. There once was a medieval monk who persistently mispronounced Latin *sumpsimus* "we have taken" as *mumpsimus* in the Latin Eucharist. Whether from ignorance or illiteracy, when the mistake was pointed out to him, his response was remarkable. The monk firmly stated that he had pronounced this word the same way for 40 years and added, "I will not change my old *mumpsimus* for your new *sumpsimus*." With this statement he carved a place for his new word in lexical history, simultaneously girding it with its singular meaning: people like the monk himself. True or not, this story is the best etymologists have come up with.

Namby-pamby • *Noun*

Pronunciation: næm-bee-pæm-bee

Outside the US, **namby-pamby** refers to a sentimentally insipid or childish person. In the US a namby-pamby is a weak-kneed, fearful, and indecisive person, someone lacking in willpower.

It should come as no surprise to anyone that many whimsical derivations have devolved naturally from this word. We might expect the adjective *namby-pambyish* and the noun, *namby-pambiness* (watch for the shift of Y to I). However, various writers have suggested namby-pambical "like a namby-pamby" and a noun, namby-pambics "the behavior of a namby-pamby."

Although the meaning of this word is demeaning, the humor in it reduces its bite, allowing it to be used on friends and loved ones: "Ben and Eileen Dover are such namby-pambies they never go to baseball games for fear of being hit by a foul ball." Outside the US, this word can apply to people who are simply mushy and sentimental: "That old namby-pamby loves watching old romantic movies on the classic movie channel."

Namby-pamby began its life as a disparaging imitation of a childish pronunciation of the first name of Ambrose Philips (1675-1749), author of sentimental poems for and about children. Philips was ridiculed by Henry Carey and Alexander Pope, especially in Carey's satiric poem *Namby Pamby*, which appeared in 1726. The word is a rhyming compound, a particularly whimsical kind of wordplay that combines a real word with a nonsense word that rhymes with it. We've seen such in *collywobbles, flibbertigibbet, fuddy-duddy,* and *hocus-pocus* so far, but dozens of others lounge about the English lexicon.

Nincompoop • *Noun*

Pronunciation: ning-kum-poop

Nincompoop is an affectionate synonym for *simpleton, dunce, fool,* and similar such deprecative terms referring to low mental capacity.

Sometimes people you love do foolish things that do not disturb your affection for them. This word is just the word you need for such situations. Nincompoops are nincompoopish people who behave nincompoopishly. If you engage in nincompoopery on a regular basis, you could achieve the awesome status of nincompoophood! Wow!

This word represents a means of calling someone foolish pleasantly, in a way suggestive of forgiveness: "Oh, no! The old nincompoop has put his trousers on backwards again!" English playwright William Wycherley used it differently in his 1676 play, *The Plain Dealer*: "Thou senseless, impertinent, quibbling, drivelling, feeble, paralytic, impotent, fumbling, frigid nincompoop." (Was it something I said?)

An earlier 16th century word, *noddypoop*, may have influenced this word, which first appeared in print in 1673. *Nincompoop* is a compound of *ninny*, a reduction of *innocent*, + *poop*. *Poop* began its career referring to the rear (aft) of a ship (as in poop deck) and ended up referring to the hinder parts of people. By the 16th century, a poop was a toot on a horn or a blast of air through a horn, but by 1744 it referred to a blast of gas from the poop deck of a person. Virginia Woolfe seems to have first published *poop* indicating a bore or stupid person in her novel *Voyage Out* (1915). We assume a nincompoop to be superior to a plain poop.

Oocephalus • *Noun*

Pronunciation: Oh-oh-**sef**-uh-lus

An **oocephalus** is an egghead, a person or animal with an egg-shaped head.

Egghead has taken on such a pejorative sense, we need to find a more civil term for the concept. *Oocephalus* seems appropriate since only egg-heads (that is, oocephali) will understand it. Notice that both Os are pronounced: not like *oo* in *kook,* but like the interjection for an accident, "Oh-oh!" The adjective, meaning "having an egg-like head," is pronounced the same way as the noun, but is spelled *oocephalous.* You may use *oocephali* or *oocephaluses* as a plural. Oocephali prefer the former.

We have been trying to discourage offensive speech for years and even if this word is not less offensive than *egghead,* at least it is less comprehensible: "The R. Cain I know is a nerdy oocephalus who spends all his time in the library collecting dust with the books there." We can now replace the fun of the insult with the fun of pronouncing this word: "Some oocephalus who has never done real work wrote the safety rules requiring that (1) construction vehicles make an audible signal when they back up and (2) all workmen wear earplugs on construction sites."

This funny word is a medical creation from Greek oion "egg" + kephale "head" + a Latinate suffix. *Oion* came from the Proto-Indo-European root awi "bird," which also produced Latin avis "bird," the origin of English *avian* and *aviary.* The Old Iranian word for "egg," *avya,* also came from this stem. It underwent several changes before Turkish adopted it as *havyar.* French then borrowed the Turkish word as *caviar,* the name of those salty fish eggs with the even saltier price.

༒

Ornery • *Adjective*

Pronunciation: or-nur-ee

Ornery means contrary, cantankerous, mean, disagreeable.

This odd little word sounds awfully American but, in fact, it came to us from 17th century England. That is long enough for it to have picked up a noun, *orneriness*, but not an adverb. Despite its longevity, it is still considered slang, so save it for humorous occasions.

Ornery is an ordinary word you are liable to hear frequently around the house in some regions: "Now, don't get ornery. Mow the lawn before the game starts; otherwise, you know it won't be done." We've all heard this low-brow word and, if I'm not mistaken, most of us occasionally use it in constructions like this: "Don't even ask Bob Wire. He is in one of his ornery moods and wouldn't give you air in a jug right now."

Words are like kids: they get into trouble easily. This word has been naughty enough to have done itself quite a bit of damage. It started out as the ordinary word *ordinary* but then, by repeated misuse and mispronunciation, turned sour in both sound and meaning. *Ordinary* came to us via French from Latin ordinarius "in order, usual, regular," an adjective based on ordo, ordinis "row, line, series." The same deep root, Proto-Indo-European ar- "fit together, join," also underlies *arm*, a word borrowed from Latin armus "upper arm." In Greek it emerged in harmos "joint, shoulder," at the root of harmonia "fitting together, harmony," which we borrowed as *harmony*. Such a long journey to end up with such a mean meaning.

Pandiculation • *Noun, mass*

Pronunciation: pæn-di-kyuh-**lay**-shun

No, **pandiculation** doesn't mean acting like a panda; in fact, it has nothing to do with pandas except right after they wake up. This funny word refers the full body stretch, stretching the entire body simultaneously, including the jaws.

This roundly needed word is about to leave us. It has already vanished from the Merriam-Webster and American Heritage dictionaries, even though we have no substitute that distinguishes the full body stretch from partial ones. *Pandiculation* is the noun from *pandiculate*, which means that someone who pandiculates must be a pandiculator.

Here is a good word to put into play in a rich variety of situations. At home you might try: "Honey, the rampant pandiculation in your audience suggests we may have seen enough of your slides." Can't you just hear this word hard at work at work? "Most of the activity on my shift is pandiculation."

English snapped this funny word up from French, which inherited it from Latin pandiculari "to stretch oneself," an extension of pandere "to spread, unfold." The past participle of *pandere* is *passus*, a root we see in *passage*, something that can also stretch quite a way. Leaves, too, stretch out as they grow, so Greek derived its word *petalos* "leaf" from this same root, minus the Fickle N, an N that comes and goes mysteriously in Indo-European words. We, of course, borrowed the Greek word as English *petal*. In Old Germanic the same original root emerged as fathmaz "an arm-spread," a word that came to English as *fathom*, now a standard nautical measure of length equal to about 6 feet long.

Panjandrum • *Noun*

Pronunciation: pæn-**jæn**-drum

Panjandrum is a mock title for a high-ranking, super supercilious, self-centered person: a big wheel, a big cheese, a Pooh-bah (the character in *The Mikado*), a High Muck-a-muck (from Chinook jargon hayo makamak "plenty to eat").

This is a word bereft of lexical kinsfolk other than a normal plural, *panjandrums*. Of course, since it ends on -um, like *datum* (plural *data*) and *paramecium* (plural *paramecia*), we might play with "all the panjandra" to get a wider smile.

This light-hearted word also has quite a bit of beauty that should not be ignored: "Today I am the Grand Panjandrum of my demesne, overseeing the fall colors of my garden, feasting on olives, cheese, grapes, and fresh-baked bread in my royally favorite nightgown." A large dahlia could be the grand panjandrum of the garden itself. This word is a fine blade to use against self-importance. "Why should I have to lay down a bunt? You're just the coach; you're not the Grand Panjandrum of Poobabia," would be a sparkling note on which to end your baseball career.

The Irish actor Charles Macklin (1699-1797) loved to boast that he could memorize any paragraph on one reading. To test that boast, Samuel Foote composed a highly nonsensical paragraph to test Macklin in 1754 (look for it in the Appendix). Macklin refused to perform with the words of Foote in his mouth. Still, one phrase in the test, "the great Panjandrum," stuck in the language, probably because it is very remindful of the names of the lords of India and Pakistan, giving it the ring of authenticity with just a touch of mystery.

Pettifogger • *Noun*

Pronunciation: pe-di-fah-gur

Originally, a **pettifogger** was an unscrupulous lawyer but later the meaning of this word migrated to anyone who quibbles over trivial details in order to obscure the meaning of what is being said or written.

The fault of the pettifogger is pettifoggery, which is generated when a pettifogger is pettifogging. If the verb is too short for you, a figure no less prominent than Thomas de Quincy has used *pettifogulize* to refer to the same activity. As late as 1932 Virginia Woolf, using the British spelling, claimed that de Quincy was himself "the prince of Pettifogulisers."

Television has raised pettifoggery to a high art, giving deft pettifoggers a bully pulpit: "The unfortunately televised debate on environmental issues was reduced to quibbling between two pettifoggers over timber rights." The US Department of State has earned itself the nickname "Foggy Bottom," probably more as a result of the amount of pettifoggery associated with it than the mistiness of its location.

Pettifogger seems to belong to the family of fanciful coinages from the US frontier, in company with *hornswoggle, gobbledygook*, and *snollygoster*. *Pettifogger*, however, is of much older vintage. It comes from the German surname, Fugger, a family of wealthy but widely disliked financiers in 15th-16th century Augsburg. A *petty Fugger* originally was a petty but deceptive businessman. When the phrase became a word, English folk etymology shifted the *fug-* to *fog*, thereby influencing the sense of the word. This new sense of someone who fogs up the discussion easily migrated to lawyers.

Pratfall • *Noun*

Pronunciation: præt-fawl

A **pratfall** is a fall on the bum, bottom, rear, butt, or a mortifying blunder, an inexcusable act of stupidity.

Although *prat* originally referred to the human rear end, today it generally refers to a foolish person or someone who has just done something foolish: "Take the lampshade off your head, you prat!" It fits anywhere the A-word goes but reflects a speaker with a richer vocabulary. It is far more common in the UK and Australia than in the US.

The original pratfall was featured in the slapstick comedies of the 20s, a quick fall backward on the cushion apparently created for just such occasions: "Sue Dasitti wasn't watching the black ice on the sidewalk and did a perfect pratfall in front of her date." However, because of the rate of population growth, metaphorical pratfalls must be much more common: "Telling the entire office that he had seen the boss's wife in Vegas with the new CFO turned out to be a major pratfall in I. Malone's short if spicy career at the company."

No one seems to know where the noun *prat* came from but its meaning seems to have originated in underworld argot. It is suspiciously identical in form to Scottish prat "cunning trick, prank." This noun was *prœt* in Old English and it had an adjective prættig "tricky, wily, crafty." The adjective today is *pretty*. This ancestor of *prat* disappeared from published works until 1478. Did it pick up a new, less acceptable meaning during this period? This would explain why the meaning of *pretty* now is so far removed from that of *prat*. However, since we have no written record of this trail of changes, we can only surmise that it occurred.

Quean • *Noun*

Pronunciation: kween

A **quean** is a floozy, a hussy, a harlot, slut, slattern, strumpet, tart, or any bold, impudent girl or woman. In fact, an effeminate gay male will do for this word. (*Queen* is an understandable US misspelling in this sense.) As always, Scotland is the exception: in some of its dialects a quean is a normal young girl.

What a difference an A makes! The semantic spread between *queen* and *quean* could not be greater, from a woman of the highest repute to one of the lowest. The adjective *queanish* (adverb *queanishly*) means "like a quean, in a queanly manner." *Queanry* is the stuff queans are made of.

This lexical golden oldie can lead to some very humorous mis-understandings if not used with care: "Heidi Fleiss was the queen of Hollywood queans until her arrest." The possibilities for word-play are endless: "*La cage aux folles* is a hilarious movie set in a night club that sponsors a nightly beauty quean pageant."

In Old English cwene "woman" and cwen "queen" were pro-nounced differently even though they were derived from the same Old Germanic word, *kweniz*. The root of this word goes back to Proto-Indo-European gwen- "woman," which emerged in Greek as gyne "woman," the root of English *gynecology*. In Russian the same PIE word emerged as zhena "wife" and, in Persian, zan "woman." In Irish Gaelic this root became bean "woman" which is used with sídhe "fairy" in the phrase bean sídhe "wailing female spirit." English collapsed this phrase into one word, *banshee*.

Rambunctious • *Adjective*

Pronunciation: ræm-**bungk**-shus

Rambunctious means noisily overactive, aggressive, outspoken, and mildly rip-roarious.

This word is a facetious concoction that managed to stick to the language like oatmeal to the ribs. It is currently an integral part of English as evidenced by its derivational kin such as the adverb *rambunctiously* and the noun *rambunctiousness*.

Kids are most often accused of rambunctiousness, especially by baby-sitters: "Sorry about the goldfish bowl, Mrs. McGillicutty; the kids were a little rambunctious tonight." However, adults have problems with it, too: "Frank became a bit rambunctious on the way home from the party last night and I had to handcuff him to the car door."

At the bottom of this word lies *robust*. Here is how it happened to become *rambunctious*. First, *robust* came from the same root that gave English *red* and *ruby*. It also emerged in Latin as robus "red oak" and this word ended up in English as *robust*. However, *robust* sounds a little weak for its definition, so someone kicked it up a notch or two to *robustious* in the 1540s. Next, some ancient mariner, no doubt, decided that a drop of rum would strengthen it even more, so converted it to *rumbustious* in the 1780s. Now, rams are very robust animals, so the Temperance ladies (my guess would be) removed the rum from this word when they were removing it everywhere else, replacing it with *ram*, giving us this word, *rambunctious* by the 1850s. I've done my share; I will let you figure why the ST became NCT.

Ranivorous • *Adjective*

Pronunciation: ruh-**ni**-vuh-rus

In a word, **ranivorous** means frog-eating, usually referring to frogs as a dietary item on the menus of larger species.

You probably thought this word applied only to a small circle of animals. Guess what? Europeans are ranivorous, too, a debt we may owe to the French, who long ago discovered the delicacy of flavor in bullfrog legs. The adverb would be *ranivorously* and the noun, *ranivorousness* rather than *ranivorosity*. Creatures that eat frogs are ranivores.

Biologists are worried about the world-wide disappearance of frogs that cannot be attributed to ranivorous species or French epicures. Many believe that frogs are a sentinel species, an early warning of a failure in our ecosystem that will mean more mosquitoes and other insects, and fewer ranivorous animals like minks, otters, raccoons, and snakes. The details are still being worked out.

This funny word comes from a compound based on Latin rana "frog" + vorare "to swallow whole, devour" + *-ous*, an English adjective suffix borrowed from Latin. *Rana* is a descendant of the Proto-Indo-European root rek- "to bellow," which is also behind Latin rancare "to bellow" and Russian rech' "speech," which omits the always expendable Fickle N. Latin *vorare* apparently devolved from a PIE root like *gwor-*, with an initial G that was lost in Latin and Greek, where we find bi-brosko "to devour." In Sanskrit we find the G in girati "s/he gobbles" and the ZH in Russian zhreti "devour, gobble" can be explained by an earlier G in that word.

Rigmarole • *Noun, mass*

Pronunciation: rig-muh-rol or **ri**-guh-muh-rol

Rigmarole is double talk, rambling, disconnected speech. It also means red tape, or some other complicated and confusing process.

The original pronunciation of this jolly word contained only one A, but most dictionaries have given up the fight to keep the second one out. If you like to speak 'original' English, resist the temptation to insert an extra A in this word after the G. However, you are in good company if you don't. The noun expressing the quality of rigmarole is *rigmarolery* and you have your choice of two adjectives: *rigmarolish* or *rigmarolic*.

If you think this word sounds a bit slangy, remember that Lord Byron thought it a word of learned speakers. In *Don Juan* (1818) he wrote, "His speech was a fine sample, on the whole, of rhetoric, which the learn'd call 'rigmarole'." Today, of course, it is fair game for speakers of all educational levels: "The registration rigmarole for a marriage license was so dismaying, we decided to call off the wedding and remain just friends."

This funny word is an alteration of obsolete *Ragman Roll* from the name of a set of scrolls given to King Edward I in 1291 by Scottish noblemen who signed deeds of loyalty to which the King affixed his seal. All these deeds were eventually joined together to produce the 12-meter long Ragman Roll, found now in the Public Records Office in London—a pretty long piece of red tape, indeed. *Ragman* comes from an old Scandinavian word referring to the Devil, a meaning the word bore in English until the 14th century. This sense of *ragman* could be a reduction of *ragged man*, where *ragged* refers to the shagginess of animals, an attribute often applied to the Devil.

Shenanigan • *Noun*

Pronunciation: shuh-**naen**-uh-gun

A **shenanigan** is a trick or annoying practical joke, perhaps a mischievous prank. It usually implies some kind of underhanded scheme or machination.

Although it starts out on the feminine personal pronoun *she*, folks of both genders are capable of shenanigans—which reminds me, this word is used more often in the plural than in the singular. It is not only a lexical orphan, with no related derivations, but an eccentric one at that, a word to which other words probably would not admit kinship. Shenanigans are something people are usually up to when they are up to no good.

Will we ever know what kind of shenanigans on the part of Wall Street financiers led to the financial meltdown of 2008? When anything of value is at stake, shenanigans are something you would want to cut out: "Cut out the shenanigans with the cards up your sleeve, Sharkey, and let's play serious poker."

This funny word sounds a lot like *she-nanny* and goats are associated with crankiness if not prankishness. A nanny, however, is a she-goat, so *she-nanny* is an unlikely combination. *Shenanigan* was first recorded in 1855 in California, which has led some to think that it is Spanish chanada "trick" with a very un-Spanish *-igan* on the end. It sounds much more like German schinaglen "to trick," but very few Germans went to California during the Gold Rush so a Germanic influence is unlikely. In all probability this word is another gift of our Irish ancestors, Gaelic sionnachuighim "I play the fox" or "I play tricks," maybe with just a thought of *she-nanny*.

Sialoquent • *Adjective*

Pronunciation: sai-æ-luh-kwint

You aren't going to believe this: **sialoquent** means spitting while talking! Sputtering saliva while chatting!

According to the Oxford English Dictionary, *sialoquent* was first listed in Thomas Blount's dictionary, *Glossographia*, published in 1656. I don't think it was given a fair chance since and I have chosen to include it in this volume in an attempt to give it one. The adverb, of course, is *sialoquently* and the noun, *sialoquence*. Pronounce it carefully.

The foremost sialoquent character in American mythology is the cartoon character Daffy Duck: "Daffy Duck is so sialoquent, there isn't a dry eye in the house when he speaks." Few humans actually speak sialoquently except under extraordinary circumstances: "Frank Palaver, sialoquently sputtering as he does after a few drinks, pelted his colleagues with harsh words and moisture, neither of which they appreciated."

This funny word is a compound some wag created from Greek sialon "spittle" + Latin loquen(t)s "speaking," the present participle of loqui "to speak." Some etymologists have tried to relate *sialon* with German *Speichel* and English *spit*, but without a convincing explanation of what happened to the P in Greek. As for *loqui*, there was a Proto-Indo-European word tolkw- "speak," which ended up in English *talk* and Russian tolkovat' "to interpret." It is possible that the O and L underwent metathesis (switched places) in early Latin, resulting in a root *tlokw-*. Were this to have occurred, the initial T would have disappeared since Latin did not permit TL at the beginning of a word. The final result would be a word spelled *loqui* and pronounced [lokwi].

Skedaddle • *Verb, intransitive*

Pronunciation: skuh-**dæd**-ul

Skedaddle is bit of humorous US slang that means to run away very hurriedly, to scoot away rapidly.

In some areas of the US South, the accent is placed on the initial syllable of this word [**skee**-dæd-ul]. However, this pronunciation today is a bit silly, since it implies an outdated southwestern rural accent. *Skedaddle* is a lexical orphan; no one has dared create a derivation of this lexical eccentricity.

Remember that this word is not only slang, but a peculiar regional slang word at that. You would be more likely to hear this down south in the US: "The kids all skedaddled when they saw you driving up. I think they thought that, since it is Saturday, you would give them all chores." Like the verb *go*, this word is intransitive, which means you cannot skedaddle anything, not even a cowboy: "The fox skedaddled out of the henhouse when cowboy Bob came in to gather the eggs."

This US lexical peculiarity arose during the Civil War. It is a playful distortion of *scuttle*, which mean "to run away hastily." The earlier form of this word is s*cuddle*, an emphatic form of the rather poetic verb *scud*, as in clouds scudding along the horizon. *Scud* may be a variant of scut "rabbit's tail," given English similes like "quick as a rabbit" and "run like a rabbit." However, it is more probably a variant of an Old Norse word for "shoot," along the lines of Modern Norwegian skudd "shot" or a derivation of a related word in Old English sceotan "to shoot."

Skullduggery • *Noun, mass*

Pronunciation: skul-**dug**-uh-ree

Skullduggery means chicanery, trickery, shadiness, underhandedness, wicked jiggery-pokery, or hanky-panky.

Given the sense of the original word (for which see below), the current meaning of this funny word is very mild in comparison to its funny look and sound. In the US, one of the Ls is often omitted (*skulduggery*) but most dictionaries now assert *skullduggery* to be the preferred spelling. Just remember that this word has double double consonants.

Using *skullduggery* instead of sterner words like *moral turpitude* or *deceit* is a way to refer to moral depravity more obliquely, more tongue-in-cheek: "What sort of skullduggery did you have to resort to in order to coax Able Mann away from the Acme Widget Company?" It may be used in a sterner sense though: "The Watergate burglary was but the final twist of a long history of political skullduggery leading up to the US elections of 1972."

This word is probably an alteration of Scots *sculduddery* "obscenity, fornication." No one has any idea where it comes from, not even the Scots. When I hear *skullduggery*, though, I think of pirates and buccaneers, whose symbol was the skull and crossbones and who were known for digging holes (*dig, dug, dug*) to bury treasure. Since *skullduggery* approaches more closely their behavior than the meaning of *skulduddery*, I think piratical influence must have been involved somewhere in the historical development of *skullduggery*.

Slangwhanger • *Noun*

Pronunciation: slæng-whæng-gur

We have no difficulty in remembering that **slangwhanger** is a slang word since it begins with a reminder. A slangwhanger is a loud, abusive speaker or an obnoxiously offensive writer.

This funny word is one I accidentally stumbled across in the Oxford English Dictionary, a lovely place for word-lovers to stumble around. There is no question of its origin: it is another comical gift of the US frontier. Its absence from US dictionaries indicates that it has faded from our collective memory just when we need it the most. What do slangwhangers do? Why slang-whang, naturally, since they are defined by their slangwhang.

Slangwhangers are usually vituperative people who take delight in affronting those they dislike: "I love to listen to the slang-whangers on the so-called political talk shows on TV." Slang-whangers generally turn every issue into a political one: "The town meeting to discuss the placement of the new school water fountains was disrupted by slangwhangers, who apparently don't drink anything as soft as water themselves."

Although this funny word sounds like a nonsense word, it does have a history. It is, just as it appears to be, a compound made up of *slang* and *whang*. *Slang* now refers to substandard or 'low' speech, but it originally referred to the vulgar speech of disrepu-table characters. *Whang* goes back to Old English *thwong*, which split into *thong* and *whang* somewhere between Old and Modern English. *Thong* originally referred to a lash and in Scotland this meaning continued in whang "to lash with a thong." (Scotland was a major source of early US settlers.) So the original meaning of this silly word was "someone who lashes out with vulgar speech"—very close to what it means today.

Smellfungus • *Noun*

Pronunciation: smel-**fung**-gus

A **smellfungus** is a fault-finder, a disagreeable curmudgeon who finds fault in everything, someone who loves misery and sharing it with others.

The plural of this good if cranky word is *smellfungi* [smel-**fun**-jee] and it is still used by those familiar with the Sterne-Smollett debate over the relative merits of France and Italy (for which see below) and other discerning conversationalists. It is a lexical oddity you might find amusing and useful in view of the dearth of politically correct terms for such people these days.

Smellfungi are bitterly egotistical people addicted to themselves to the point of constant wretchedness: "That old smellfungus could find fault in the very saints!" By implication, such people become a misery to those who know them, "Farthingsworth is a smellfungus who finds enough misery in the world for himself and all his acquaintances."

This lexical oddity is fallout, believe it or not, from a dispute over the relative merits of France and Italy. Tobias Smollett's collection of letters entitled *Travels through France and Italy* (1766) is remarkable for its persistent criticism of those two countries. Laurence Sterne referred to Smollett as "the learned Smelfungus" in his more sympathetic appraisal of the region in 1767 entitled *A Sentimental Journey through France and Italy*. Apparently Sterne felt that Smollett could smell a fungus even where none existed and hence created this funny word to the delight of others. The word has since picked up an additional L and found a snug niche for itself in the speech of discriminating logophiles.

Snickersnee • *Noun*

Pronunciation: snik-ur-snee

Snickersnee has two meanings: a large or long knife or a Dutch method of fighting with large knives.

This absurdity of this word prevents it from developing any derivational relatives. It is pronounced pretty much the way it is spelled. *Snickersnee* may be used as a noun or as a verb meaning "to fight with a snickersnee": "Smedley discovered quickly that he could not snickersnee the rapidly approaching grizzly bear."

In Act II of *The Mikado*, Gilbert and Sullivan could not resist the humor in this word: "The criminal cried, as he dropped him down.... As he squirmed and struggled, And gurgled and guggled, I drew my snickersnee, My snickersnee!" Today, however, this word is used only figuratively. As late as 1976, according to the October 18 issue of *Newsweek*, Howard W. Smith, a Virginia Democrat, defended his use of the House Rules Committee chairmanship to block civil-rights legislation by quipping, "[Y]ou grasp any snickersnee you can get hold of and fight the best way you can."

This fascinating and funny word is a compound that originated as a phrase, to stick and snee "to cut and thrust in a knife fight." Until the middle of the 19th century the two activities had discrete names. The phrase itself is a moderate corruption of Dutch steken en snijden "stab and cut" from steken "to stab" + en "and" + snijden "to cut," with the N of *snijden* carrying over and replacing the T in *stecken*. *Steken* is related to German stechen "to stick, stab" and English *stick*. *Snijden* comes from the same source as German Schneider "tailor" and Schnitzel "cutlet," as in *Wiener schnitzel*, which English picked up from German.

Snollygoster • *Noun*

Pronunciation: snah-li-gah-stur

Snollygoster or **snallygaster** was originally the name of a monster that preyed on poultry and children—an odd combination to be sure. Today, however, it more often indicates a rotten person who is driven by greed and self-interest. I do have reports from New England, however, that this word is used in some areas up there to refer to terrible storms that hit the Eastern Seaboard. For sure this word always refers to something nasty.

There are no relatives of this word. The two spellings might reflect the possibility of both O and A representing the sound [ah]. This would make sense since *snallygaster* would have been the earlier spelling, when most Americans spoke with British accents. As US English developed, we would expect the spelling to change to *snollygoster*, which seems to have been the case.

I like this word as a term for a horrible storm but that sense seems to be narrowly limited to a small region in the US. More generally it refers to an amoral man: "That old snollygoster who runs this company just cut our lunch hour down to 20 minutes!" In the US those of us who use this word tend to focus it on ruthless politicians: "Those who complain about politicians today should recall the real snollygosters like New York's Boss Tweed back in the 19th century."

We only know for sure that *snollygoster* is a US dialectal creation that might possibly have come from Pennsylvania Dutch (German) schnelle geeschter "fast spirits, ghosts." This phrase is the equivalent of German *schnelle Geister* with the same meaning. German Geist "spirit, ghost" is a cousin of English *ghost*, and is found in two English borrowings from German, poltergeist "noisy ghost" and zeitgeist "spirit of the times." But this stem is rarely found outside the Germanic languages; it is like, well, a ghost of a word.

Snool • *Noun*

Pronunciation: snool

A **snool** is a coward, a milquetoast, a drudge; a servile person who submits tamely to oppression.

This word holds no spelling or pronunciation traps. It is a lexical orphan without a derivational family. It may be used as a verb: *to snool* is more natural to English than the Chinese word *kow-tow*. It is a useful substitute for all those horrible phrases, such as *to brown-nose* and *to suck up to*, which have unpleasant associations.

Because of its alliteration with words like *snot, snivel*, and *snoot*, this word is an ear-catching substitute for words like *sycophant* and *brown-noser*. "Oh, I would say that Ben Dover is more than just a yes-man; I would say that he is more a sniveling driveling snool who enjoys the boss's abasement day in and day out." His sister, Eileen, is just as bad; she snools through life with bovine equanimity.

This funny word, like much English lexical humor, comes from Scotland and the northern English dialects. It is a dialectal variant of *snivel* as *drool* is a variant of *drivel*. *Snivel* is from Old English snofl "mucus," probably borrowed from Danish snøvle "to sniffle"; indeed, *sniffle* is a close relative. Both these words are related to snuff "to draw up the nostrils," of which only the noun *snuff* remains in active use, aside from the usage of the verb in the criminal argot meaning "to murder."

Tatterdemalion • *Noun*

Pronunciation: tæt-ur-duh-may-lyun

A **tatterdemalion** is a ragamuffin (no sedate expression itself), a person in dirty or raggedy clothes, usually a child.

This word is a lexical orphan presenting no pronunciation or spelling pitfalls other than in its length. It is a jaunty word that lies in danger of being ignored right out of the language, so consider this a call to rescue it.

We usually associate raggedness with poverty: "Aurora, my little darling, I would prefer that you play with someone other than the tatterdemalions down at the public playground." The fact of the matter is, however, the tatterdemalion look has become quite fashionable today, though some parents fail to keep up with the styles: "Lucy, don't go out looking like a tatterdemalion; you have jeans without holes in them to wear to school."

This eccentric word is the *tatter* in the phrase *in tatters*, followed by a factitious, rather Frenchy element suggesting that the word might be an ethnic derivation (it isn't). *Tatter* is of Scandinavian origin, no doubt brought in by one of the Viking invasions of northern England from the 9th to 11th centuries. It is very similar to Old Norse *taturr* which shows up later in Icelandic *töturr* [ö = e with your lips puckered] "tatters, rags." A similar form has been reported in Norwegian dialects as *totra*. Theories about the origin of the remainder of the word, *-demalion*, are themselves in tatters.

Troglodyte • *Noun*

Pronunciation: trahg-luh-dait

A **troglodyte** is a person who lives in a cave or building carved into a hillside. Since such people set themselves apart from others, the word also came to refer to a reclusive, anachronistic person who resists change. Finally, this word can also indicate a pongid, such as a gorilla, orangutan, or chimpanzee.

This curious word has a limited immediate family, only an adjective *troglodytic*. The first constituent, *troglo-*, may be combined with other Greek words to create new words like troglophile "a cave-lover or cave-dwelling animal." And, if *troglophile*, why not troglophobe "someone who fears caves." Looks OK to me.

You probably never thought of chimpanzees as troglodytes yet their scientific name is *pan troglodytes*, perhaps from the days when we thought they lived in caves. But this word is used most widely in the sense of an anachronistic recluse: "Nothing brings the troglodytes out of the woodwork like the smell of change." I suppose your attitude toward change will determine whether you identify with the troglodytes or the change-makers.

Let us see if we can dig out the origin of this word. It was kidnapped pretty much as is from Greek *troglodytes*, which referred to animals that live in holes, such as mice, foxes, and snakes. Later on it was applied to cavemen. In Greek the word was a compound from trogle "gnawed hole" (from trogein "to gnaw") + dytes "one who enters." ("Cave" in Greek was *spelunx*, from which we derive *spelunker*.) But troglodytes to the Greeks were also Caucasian or Middle Eastern peoples who carved their homes in rocks or lived in decorated caves. Aristotle referred to troglodytes as midgets and thought that they fought wars against cranes (the birds).

Turdiform • *Adjective*

Pronunciation: tur-duh-form

Turdiform means shaped like or resembling a thrush.

If you would feel a little awkward using this funny word in conversations with your friends, there are two other variants with the same meaning, *turdoid* and *turdine*. All these adjectives can also mean "belonging to the family turdus," as do the song-thrush (Turdus musicus) and Santa's favorite, the mistletoe thrush (Turdus viscivorus), among others. If you are a genuine thrush-fancier, you will want to keep your thrushes in a specially constructed turdarium. However, if you put other varieties in with your thrushes, you can't call it that any more.

This is a good word with which to attract attention to yourself in discussions with bird-watchers: "I saw an interesting little turdiform flyer in my backyard yesterday but it was green and pileated. Have any idea what it might have been?" The many types of birds that resemble thrushes provide plenty of work for this word: "Do you happen to know the name of the lovely little turdiform creature sitting on the birdfeeder right now?"

This rather startling word comes from a Latin compound based on turdus "thrush" + forma "form." The root of *turdus* started out as trozdos "thrush," but in Latin the [r] and the vowel metathesized, i.e. changed places. Among the Germanic languages these two sounds held their positions and produced English *thrush*, German Drossel "thrush," with the diminutive suffix *-el*, and the Russian word, drozd "thrush."

Unremacadamized • *Participle*

Pronunciation: un-ree-muh-kæ-duh-maizd

This rather long word means "having not been covered again with crushed stone, tar, or asphalt."

One of the most fascinating aspects of the English language is the extent to which it reflects the melting pots of the English-speaking nations. This word is a lexical Dagwood sandwich with an English prefix and suffix holding chunks of four other languages together. The prefix un- "not" and the past participle suffix -*ed* are pure English. Between them we find the Latin prefix re- "again," the Scots Gaelic prefix mac "son of" from *McAdam*, the inventor of macadam, the Hebrew word adam "man" and, finally, -*ize*, the Greek verbal suffix found in words like arch**aize**in "to be old fashioned."

Conceivable situations calling for this improbable word do arise: "Our street remained unremacadamized for decades until the head of the Department of Transportation bought a house on it." Of course, anyone living in an invious (roadless) region would be envious of even an unremacadamized road.

The root of this good word has an eponym in the name of John Loudon McAdam (1786-1836), a Scotsman who built roads with crushed stone bound with gravel on a firm base of larger stones. Because McAdam curved the surfaces of his roads, water ran off to the sides without compromising the base. Travel was much faster on these roads, which came to be called 'Macadamized' roads. Much later, the crushed stone in macadamized roads was reinforced with tar, then asphalt, giving us the current reference of the word *macadam*.

Vomitory • *Noun*

Pronunciation: vah-muh-to-ree

No, this is not a dormitory on house party weekend; a **vomitory** is a tunnel or passageway leading out of the seating area of a stadium or amphitheater. In fact, a discharge outlet of any kind may be called a vomitory.

Although it may be used as an adjective referring to throwing up, as a noun this word refers only to passages or openings for the discharge of people and substances. The adjective for the noun is *vomitorial*, as in vomitorial capacity. The noun itself is sometimes replaced by the original Latin word, *vomitorium*, especially in referring to the vomitories of Greek and Roman amphitheaters.

English needs a word that names passages specifically designated to discharge spectators, so why not restore this one to its former luster? "Bill left the stadium early so as not to be crushed in a vomitory packed with fans once the game is over." However, this word fits any outlet for the discharge of pretty much anything: "During a rainstorm, downspouts become the primary vomitories of rainwater cascading down the roofs of a buildings."

This funny word is the locative noun from Latin vomitare "discharge, vomit frequently." A locative noun is a noun indicating place and *-orium* was the Latin suffix indicating the place of an activity. We also see the English version of this suffix in dormitory "sleeping place" and laboratory, literally, "work place." *Vomitare* is a variant of vomere "to discharge, vomit." In Greek the initial V disappeared, resulting in emein "to vomit." The adjective from this verb, *emetikos*, was picked up by the medical profession as *emetic*, an agent causing vomiting.

Wabbit • *Adjective*

Pronunciation: wæ-bit

Wabbit is another funny Scottish word usually used in the sense of tired, worn out, exhausted. However, it can also refer to things off-color or risqué.

I found this word carefully tucked away in pages of the *Oxford English Dictionary*. You are unlikely to find it in other dictionaries, though *Encarta* is brave enough to support it. Neither of these sources, however, tells us about its family: is the comparative *wabbiter* or *more wabbit*? I would go with the latter. May we behave *wabbitly* when suffering from *wabbitness*? We will leave these issues to your discretion.

August 5, 1973 the *Dundee (Scotland) Sunday Post* asked, "Been feeling a bit wabbit lately? Blaming it on the heat and the close, thundery weather?" Then in 1985 Margaret Truman wrote in *Murder in the Smithsonian*, "'I'm feeling a bit wabbit,' she said. 'Wabbit?' 'Not well.'" And didn't Elmer Fudd once say, after hunting Bugs Bunny for most of a cartoon, "I bewieve the wabbit is a bit wabbit." (I could be mistaken.)

We know that this word comes from that verbal oddity factory, Scotland, but I have no idea of how it arrived there. We do find an Old English word *wap* "to throw back, flap" that can't be connected to *wabbit*. An old noun woubit "wooly bear" looks a bit similar but not semantically so. We could be talking about someone in a Scottish village, so exhausted from hunting rabbits and fortifying himself along the way, that he could not talk clearly. The result was a confusion of words that led to the creation of a word so amusing that the whole village began repeating it. Weirder things have happened.

Whippersnapper • *Noun*

Pronunciation: hwi-pur-snæ-pur

A **whippersnapper** is a feisty, snippy, combative upstart, usually a young one.

This word offers little for us to explore. It is a lexical orphan and an oddity that does not lend itself to further derivation. If I were to derive a noun from it, I would choose *whippersnappery*. Nor would I be the first to do so: it currently occurs 101 times on the Web. This word is usually associated with youth and it most frequently occurs in the phrase *young whippersnapper*. Age apparently mellows whippersnappers, which might be a good thing.

As mentioned above, whippersnappery seems to be the domain of the young: "That young whippersnapper over there just called me an old fogy!" Some of you might take umbrage at the suggestion that we lose our whippersnappery as we age: "Hey guys, some old whippersnapper just broke my middle finger!" It works for me.

This word is a jingle variation of whip-snapper "a cracker of whips," influenced by dialectal snippersnapper "a conceited, insignificant fellow." You might have noticed that I love rhyming compounds like *namby-pamby, fuddy-duddy, slang-whanger, wishy-washy, willy-nilly,* and the like. (I collect them in Dr. Goodword's Office on the alphaDictionary website.) *Whippersnapper* is another member of this playful group.

Widdershins • *Adverb*

Pronunciation: wid-ur-shinz

Widdershins means moving in a direction opposite the usual way or simply counterclockwise. It can mean contrary to the course of the sun, which is considered bad luck by those who believe in the occult. It also means unlucky, cursed, ill-fated.

This word is a variant of *withershins*. The Oxford English Dictionary, in fact, prefers *withershins*, but you may use either to indicate hair standing on end: "The presence of the dog sent the cat's hair widdershins." You can make this adverb into an adjective by simply removing the S: "The widdershin hair of the cat sent the dog skedaddling."

As a predicate adjective, however, the S is sometimes left on. D. H. Lawrence wrote in *The Plumed Serpent* (1926) "She made up her mind to be alone, and to cut herself off from all the mechanical widdershin contacts....He, too, was widdershins, unwinding the sensations of disintegration and anti-life." Look for niches in your conversations where you can tuck this authentic English word in: "This has been one of those days when I feel that I have been walking widdershins up the down escalator."

This word is another wonderword from bonnie auld Kiltland that deserves wider respect. *Widdershins* goes back to Old Germanic *weddersinnes*, based on wider "back" or wither "reverse" + the genitive case of sin "way, direction." *Widder* and *wither* are akin to German wider "against" and wieder "again." *Sin* is related to Latin sentire "sense, feel," derived from the original Proto-Indo-European root sent- "go in or choose a direction." We borrowed *sense* from the noun of this verb. The same root also gave us the verb send "to cause something to go in a specific direction."

Yahoo • *Noun & Interjection*

Pronunciation: yah-hoo

Yahoo is a clod, bumpkin, hick, klutz, lout, rube, or it may be an ordinary philistine. It could be a clumsy, unsophisticated person without much learning. *Yahoo* is also an interjection, a cry of happy excitement or exultation, as in "Yahoo! I won the lottery!"

The founders of the Yahoo!® search engine apparently neglected to read *Gulliver's Travels* before picking a name for their company or they might have chosen a less ambiguous one, say, *Geronimo!* The noun, *yahoo*, is an old word for an uneducated dirt farmer. Now that farmers are as well-educated as the rest of us, the name applies to any clumsy bumpkin, from the country, city, or points in between. Yahooism "acting like a yahoo" has been tried, as well as yahoodom "all yahoos taken together." Use them at your own discretion.

This word is used as a noun most widely in reference to someone lacking any penchant for clear thinking: "Some yahoo from the Flat Earth Society wants equal time in our geography class." When the request was turned down, all the students in the geography class shouted, "Yahoo!"

The noun *yahoo* and the interjection are probably different words. The noun first appeared in Jonathan Swift's novel *Gulliver's Travels* in 1726. Yahoos in that novel were degraded humanoids used as beasts of burden by the Houyhnhnms, a race of rational horses. The interjection would seem to be a variant of *yoo-hoo* or *yo-ho*, extensions of *you* used for attracting someone's attention. It is used widely by cowboys herding cattle.

CR

 • *Symbol*

Pronunciation: æt-sain

The *at*-**sign**, as English-speakers call it, is used to indicate the rate by which a set of items is valued, for instance, to buy two pounds of tomatoes @ (at) $5 a pound. It is also used as an indicator of an e-mail address, e.g. 2bad@donttrythis.org, separating the account name from the domain name.

@ is a symbol widely used in English that does not have a special name as do the ampersand, semicolon, and period. We call it the *at*-sign because it symbolizes the word *at* in price quotations. In Europe, however, this symbol has taken on a myriad of highly inventive names. Fasten your seatbelts!

Most Europeans see animals in the *at*-sign. The Dutch call it an apestaart "monkey's tail" while the Germans call it a Klammeraffe "spider monkey." The Poles and Serbians also see monkeys in @: in Polish it is *małpa* and in Serbian, *majmun*, but their fellow Slavs, the Russians, see it as a little dog or *sobachka*. The Finns call it kissanhäntä "a cat's tail." In Portuguese and Spanish it is an *arroba*, a unit of weight equivalent to 15 kilograms but @ reminds some peoples of food. The Czechs call it a zavináč "rollmop." When they are hungry, Swedes see a kanelbulle "cinnamon bun" in @ but after a good meal it is just a snabel-A "elephant-trunk A." The French and Italians see snails when they see @: the French call it an *escargot* and the Italians, a *chiocciola*.

The origin of the symbol @ is the French preposition à "to, at, in" in expressions like: à 2 Euros le kilo "at 2 Euros the kilo." The grave accent over this word lengthened over time until it completely embraced the A itself. As a matter of fact, the use of *a* as a preposition meaning "per" in English expressions like "five dollars a pound" and "twenty miles an hour" came to us from French *à* way before we transmogrified it into @.

Glossary

Ablaut. A peculiarity of Proto-Indo-European languages (see below) whereby all words containing a O in their root, have a correlate with an E, as in Greek pous, pod- "foot" and Latin pes, ped- "foot." No one knows what purpose ablaut served in Proto-Indo-European (see below).

Alliteration. Consonant rhyme, the repetition of the same consonant, as in "Peter Piper picked a peck of pickled peppers."

Antonym. A word with the opposite meaning of some other word, as *black* is the antonym of *white*.

Aphaeresis The loss of an initial vowel or syllable, as in the pronunciation of *opossum* as *'possum*.

Assimilation. A consonant becoming the same as or similar to the consonant next to it, as does the N in the Latin negative prefix *in-* in words like *irrelevant, immature,* and *illegal*.

Blend. The intentional creation of a word by smushing two words together, e.g. *smoke + fog > smog, motor + hotel > motel*.

Case. Noun and adjective case is a feature of the grammars of some languages whereby the function of a noun is indicated by a distinct ending on the noun. For example, while *tabula* means "board" in Latin, "of the board" is *tabulae*.

Clipping. The shortening of a word by removing a syllable or two from the end (*doc* for *doctor*), the beginning (*van* for *caravan*) or both (*flu* for *influenza*).

Commonization. The conversion of a proper noun to a common noun, as the name Boycott became the English verb *boycott*.

Diminutive. A form of a noun that refers to a small or beloved version of the noun's meaning, as *kitty* is a diminutive of *cat*, and *duckling* is a diminutive of *duck*. English no longer produces them but they are common in languages like German, Hebrew, and Russian.

Eponym. A proper noun that becomes commonized, as Charles C. Boycott (1832-1897) is the eponym of the verb *boycott.*

Etymology. The study of the history of words undertaken by etymologists.

Euphemism. An acceptable expression used in place of an unacceptable or taboo word, such as *pee* for the four-letter word, *Gee-whiz* for "Jesus," or *golly* for "God."

Fickle N. An N ([n] sound) that comes and goes in some Proto-Indo-European words for reasons we don't understand. We find it in the Latin infinitive frangere "to break" but not in the past participle fractus "broken."

Fickle S. An S ([s] sound) found at the beginning of some Proto-Indo-European words in some languages but not others, e.g. English *slack* comes from the same root as Latin *laxus* "lax."

Folk etymology. Reanalyzing a foreign word so that it is compatible with native words, as the foreign-sounding Spanish *cucaracha* was converted into *cockroach*, made up of two English words.

Frequentative. A special form of a verb which indicates that an action is repeated more than once.

Indo-European. Related to those languages of India except for the southern tip, the languages of Iran (Persian), Pakistan, Sri Lanka, the non-native languages of the Americas, the European languages except for Estonia, Finland, Hungary, Turkey, and the Basque regions of Spain. The languages that developed from Proto-Indo-European (for which see below).

Metathesis. Two sounds switching places as in pronouncing *ask, aks* or the pronunciation of *prescription* as *perscription.*

Middle English. English spoken from the middle of the 12th century to about 1470.

Modern English. English as it is spoken today, since 1470.

Old English. The earliest form of English, spoken from the mid 5th century to the mid 12th century in what is today England and Southern Scotland.

Onomatopoeia. The creation of a word that sounds like the sound it represents, e.g. *quack, meow, crack, slosh*.

Proto-Indo-European (PIE) . An ancient language that probably existed about 5000-6000 years ago in what today is eastern Poland and western Ukraine. There are no written records of the language. It has been reconstructed from the contemporary languages of India and Europe by linguists.

Rhotacism. The conversion of an S to an R, as in Latin flos, florem "flower" and *genus, generis* "kind, type."

Rhyming compound. A compound made up of a word followed by a word that rhymes with it, such as *willy-nilly, namby-pamby, fuddy-duddy*.

Synonym. A word with the same meaning as another, as *couch* is a synonym of *sofa*.

Keep an eye open for the next book in Dr. Beard's series of Best English Words: *The 100 Most Beautiful Words in English*.

Appendix

Foote's Paragraph for Macklin

The great Irish actor Charles Macklin (1699-1797) once claimed that he could memorize anything. A fellow actor, Samuel Foote, decided to test his claim and wrote the following nonsensical paragraph and sent it to Macklin as a test:

So she went into the garden to cut a cabbage-leaf to make an apple-pie; and at the same time a great she-bear, coming up the street, pops its head into the shop. "What! No soap?" So he died, and she very imprudently married the barber; and there were present the Picninnies, and the Joblillies, and the Garyulies, and the grand Panjandrum himself, with the little round button at top, and they all fell to playing the game of catch as catch can till the gunpowder ran out at the heels of their boots.

Macklin indignantly refused to take Foote's test.

Selected References

American Heritage Dictionary of the English Language. Boston: Houghton-Mifflin Publishers, 2000.

Chantrell, Glynnis. *The Oxford Dictionary of Word Histories.* Oxford: Oxford University Press, 2002.

Encarta® World English Dictionary [North American Edition]. http://encarta.msn.com/encnet/features/dictionary/dictionary home.aspx. Redmond, Washington: Microsoft, 2009.

The Century Dictionary, ed. William Dwight Whitney. Online: http://www.global-language.com/century. New York: Century Company, 1889.

Harper, Douglas. *Etymonline.com.* http://www.etymonline.com, 2001.

Klein, Ernest. *A Comprehensive Etymological Dictionary of the English Language.* Amsterdam: North Holland, 1966.

Merriam-Webster Unabridged Dictionary. Online: http://unabridged.merriam-webster.com. Springfield, Massachusetts: Merriam-Webster, 2009.

Pokorny, Julius. *Indogermanisches Etymologisches Wörterbuch,* 3rd ed. Tübingen-Basel: Franke Verlag, 1994.

The Oxford English Dictionary. Oxford: Oxford University Press, http://www.oed.com, 2008.

Skeat, Walter. *An Etymological Dictionary of the English Language.* Mineola, New York: Dover Publications, 2005.

Made in the USA
Charleston, SC
01 April 2011